PAINT SHOP PRO 7

in easy steps

STEPHEN COPESTAKE

COMPUTER
STEP

In easy steps is an imprint of Computer Step
Southfield Road . Southam
Warwickshire CV47 0FB . England

http://www.ineasysteps.com

Reprinted 2002

Notice of Liability
Every effort has been made to ensure that this book contains accurate and current information. However, Computer Step and the author shall not be liable for any loss or damage suffered by readers as a result of any information contained herein.

Trademarks
Paint Shop Pro® is a registered trademark of Jasc Software Incorporated. All other trademarks are acknowledged as belonging to their respective companies.

Printed and bound in the United Kingdom

ISBN 1-84078-195-5

Contents

First steps

In this chapter, you'll learn how to use the Paint Shop Pro screen (including guides and grids); open existing files; create new ones (including from scanners and digital cameras); and save changes to disk. You'll rescale images, and resize the underlying canvas, then go on to learn about special screen modes. You'll also zoom in and out on images and reverse/redo image amendments. Finally, you'll learn how to work with background/foreground colours and (in the Anniversary Edition) run the Product Tour and tutorials for on-screen help.

Covers

Chapter One

The Paint Shop Pro screen

The Paint Shop Pro screen is exceptionally easy to use. When you run the program, this is the result (minus the loaded picture):

Title bar   Menu bar   Toolbar

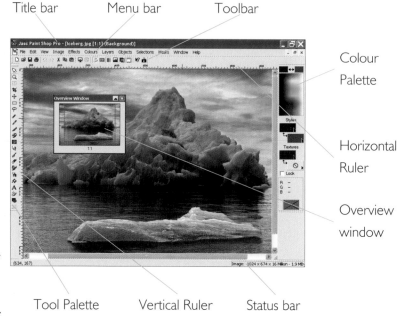

Colour
Palette

Horizontal
Ruler

Overview
window

Tool Palette   Vertical Ruler   Status bar

The other components are common to most or all Windows programs. See your Windows documentation for how to use them.

The Toolbar

This is a collection of icons. By clicking an appropriate icon, you can launch a specific feature.

Many other screen features (e.g. the Status bar, Colour Palette and Overview window) are also classed as toolbars.

For more on the Overview window, see page 20.

The Tool Palette

A specialised toolbar which you use to launch a variety of tools (e.g. the Zoom tool – see page 19).

The Colour Palette

An easy and convenient way to access Paint Shop Pro's colour selection tools (see pages 24–25).

Using guides

You can create guides in Paint Shop Pro pictures. Guides are useful alignment devices because you can ensure that:

- selections

- vector objects

- brush strokes

are automatically aligned with guides when they come within a specific distance.

Creating guides

To specify the distance at which objects snap to guides, double-click a ruler. In the dialog, type in a distance (in pixels) in the Snap influence in pixels field – the default setting is '15'. Click OK.

1 Ensure rulers are currently displayed (see page 11)

2 Ensure guides are currently displayed (see page 11)

3 Click in the vertical or horizontal ruler and drag to produce a guide

This is a horizontal guideline:

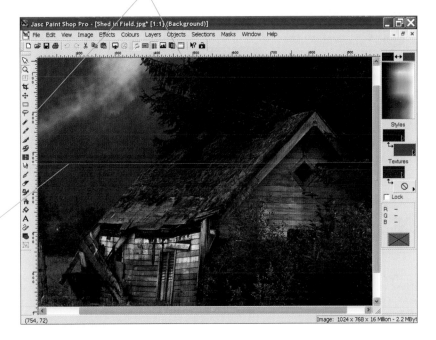

You can also have Paint Shop Pro apply a grid to images. Grids are a structure of horizontal/vertical lines which you can use to align objects more accurately:

Part of a grid

To view (or hide) the grid, press Ctrl+Alt+G.

If an image has both guides and a grid active, the grid is ignored.

To delete a guide, drag it off the image window.

To have selections/ vector objects align with guides, the Snap To Guides feature must be turned on. If it isn't, pull down the View menu and click Snap To Guides.

You can perform a variety of editing actions on existing guides.

Moving guides

Drag the handle to a new location

Recolouring guides

By default, guides may be grey or black. To apply a new colour:

1 Double-click a guide's handle

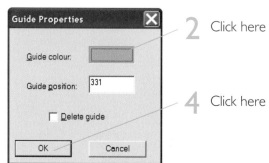

2 Click here

4 Click here

3 Refer to the Colour ring on the top right of the Colour dialog. Drag on the outer ring to select a hue, then drag the selector in the inner square to adjust the saturation. When the New colour box shows the correct colour, click OK

Customising screen components

To view or hide a toolbar, follow step 1 but select Toolbars instead. Do the following:

You can use two techniques to specify which screen components display:

Displaying the grid, guides or rulers

Pull down the View menu and do the following:

Tick or untick 1 or more toolbars, then click Close

Click Grid, Guides or Rulers

Displaying the Tool and Colour palettes

In the on-screen Toolbar, do the following as appropriate:

Step 1 also hides the Grid, Guides or Rulers, as appropriate.

To hide the Status bar, right-click the Tool Palette and select Status Bar.

Click here to show/hide the Tool palette

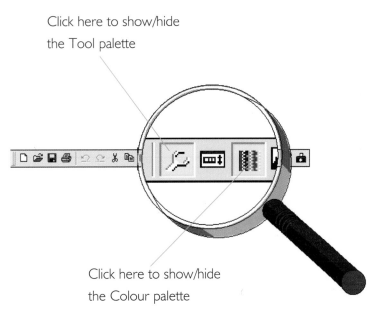

Click here to show/hide the Colour palette

Opening files

Paint Shop Pro will open (i.e. read and display) over 40 separate graphics file formats. These fall into two broad categories: raster and vector – see Chapter 8 for details of some of the principal image formats supported by Paint Shop Pro. When you tell Paint Shop Pro to open an image, it automatically recognises which format it was written to, and acts accordingly. It does this by taking account of the file suffix. For example, for TIFF (Tagged Image File Format) images to be opened in Paint Shop Pro, they must end in: .TIF

Not all of the supported formats, however, can be written to disk. (See page 18 for how to save/export files.)

You open files via the Open dialog, or via a special Browser.

Opening images – the dialog route

In the Open dialog, highlight an image and click Details for information about it before you open it.

When an image has been opened, press Shift+I for the same information. Additionally, select the Creator Information tab and enter your own image information (e.g. the artist's name and brief details).

Before you carry out step 2, carry out the following procedures:

- *use the Look in: field to locate the drive which hosts the file you want to open, and;*

- *(if necessary) double-click one or more folders until you locate the relevant file*

| Pull down the File menu and click Open

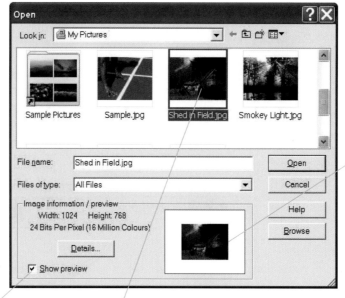

Image Preview

2 Double-click a graphics file then complete any further dialog which launches

To preview your image before you open it, ensure Show Preview is activated (as here).

...cont'd

Opening images – the Browser route

You can also use the Browser for file housekeeping. Do the following:

Press Ctrl+B if the Browser isn't on-screen. Then simply right-click any image thumbnail on the right of the Browser and do any of the following:

• to rename the image, click Rename. In the Rename File dialog, type in the new name and click OK

• to copy the image, click Copy To. In the Browse for Folder dialog, type in the destination folder and click OK, or;

• to delete the image, click Delete. In the message which appears, click Yes to confirm the deletion

To close the Browser, press Ctrl+F4.

1 Follow step 1 on the facing page

2 Carry out the procedures in the DON'T FORGET tip on the facing page

3 Click this button: Browse

Image thumbnails

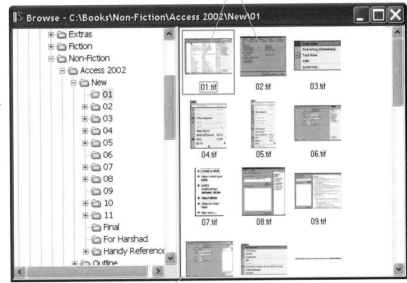

For brief image details, place the mouse pointer over a thumbnail for a few seconds – an explanatory box launches e.g.:

```
02.tif
789 x 593 x 16 Million, 270.4 KB
Tagged Image File Format
15/10/01 20:42:20
```

4 Double-click an image

Resizing files

Paint Shop Pro lets you resize an image. You can do this in three ways:

- by altering the pixel dimensions

- by restating the dimensions as a percentage of the original

- by changing the image resolution (called 'resampling')

Resizing an image

1 Pull down the Image menu and click Resize

2 Perform step 3, 4 OR 5. Finally, carry out step 6:

3 Click here, then amend the associated Width or Height fields

Re step 5 – increasing the resolution reduces the image size (and vice versa).

To select a new resizing type, click the Resize Type field. In the list, select a type.

Resizing bitmaps produces some level of distortion.

The trick is to minimise this as far as possible.

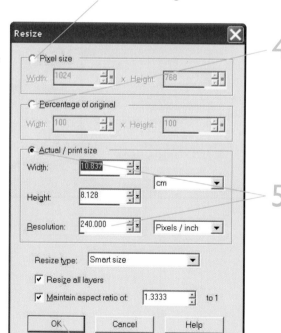

4 Click here, then amend the associated Width or Height fields

5 Click here, then type in a new resolution in the Resolution field

6 Click here

New files

Often, images will be 'ready-made' for you, in the sense that you'll:

- open existing images (see pages 12–13)

- create screenshots by carrying out screen captures (see Chapter 7)

- duplicate existing images (see the HOT TIP)

However, there will be times when you'll need to create an image from scratch. There are several stages, but Paint Shop Pro makes this easy:

1. launching the New Image dialog

2. specifying the width and height, in pixels

3. selecting a background colour

4. specifying the resolution

5. selecting an image type (including the number of colours)

Creating a new image

Pull down the File menu and do the following:

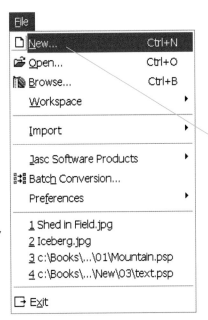

Click New (if you've already opened or created a picture, the File menu is considerably bigger)

Re step 3 – use the following suggestions as guidelines as to the correct resolution:

- *Web pictures – use a resolution of 72 pixels per inch, and;*
- *other pictures – use the range 96–150 pixels per inch (a useful standard)*

You can import new images from digital cameras directly into Paint Shop Pro. Do the following:

- *ensure the camera is connected to your PC*
- *if necessary, rerun the Installation program to install the necessary driver*
- *choose File, Import, Digital Camera, Configure, then complete the dialog (e.g. select your camera)*
- *choose File, Import, Digital Camera, Access, then review and download the relevant pictures*
- *use Paint Shop Pro's image editing facilities to refine the image. For example, if a photograph contains unwanted areas, crop it. Or remove red-eye if the subject is a person facing the lens (see pages 139–140)*

Now carry out the following steps:

2 Complete the Width and Height fields

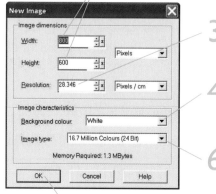

3 Optionally – specify an image resolution here

4 Click here

6 Click here

8 Click here

5 Select a background (canvas) colour

2 Colours (1 Bit)
16 Colours (4 Bit)
Greyscale (8 Bit)
256 Colours (8 Bit)
16.7 Million Colours (24 Bit)

7 Select an image type

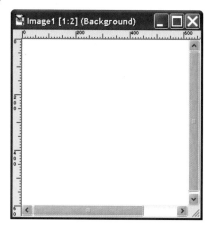

The resulting new, blank image (the background colour is white) in its own window

Enlarging an image's canvas

Enlarging an image's canvas (unlike resizing) does not expand the image itself.

As we've seen on pages 15–16, when you create an image from scratch, you specify the width and height in pixels. When you do this, Paint Shop Pro automatically defines a 'canvas' (the area on which the image lies) with the same dimensions. However, you can easily specify increased dimensions for the canvas (e.g. if you resize the image).

Increasing an image's canvas

Before you carry out steps 1–3 here, first follow step 2 under 'Using the Select Colour panel' on page 25 to select a background colour.

1 Pull down the Image menu and click Canvas Size

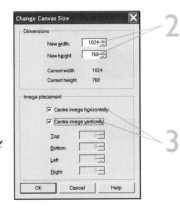

2 Complete the New Width and/or New Height fields

Re step 3 – if you don't select both centring options, also complete the relevant placement boxes:

3 Optional – select either or both of these to centre the image within the new canvas

Canvas enlargement in action:

Here, the canvas has been enlarged vertically and horizontally

In this instance, the background is white

Saving files

*Re step 1 –
Paint Shop Pro
has its own
proprietary
format (suffix:
.PSP) which retains:*

• layers

• vectors

• masks

• selection data

*Use the PSP format while
you're working with an
image; when it's complete,
save it to the nonproprietary
format of your choice.*

*See Chapter 8
for how to save
pictures for the
Web.*

*Re step 1 –
many image
formats have
sub-formats
and/or
compression options you can
choose from.*

*If it's available, click the
Options button immediately
after step 1. In the resulting
dialog, select the appropriate
option(s). Click OK.*

*The procedures
here export files
one at a time.
See page 173
for how to
export files in batches.*

When you're working on one or more images in Paint Shop Pro,
it's important to save your work at frequent intervals, in order to
avoid data loss in the event of a hardware fault or power
interruption.

Saving a file for the first time

Pull down the File menu and click Save. Now do the following:

2 Click here; in the drop-
down list, click a drive

3 Optional – double-
click 1 or more
folders

5 Click Save

4 Name the
image

1 Click here; in the list, click a format to save
to e.g. Photoshop or Encapsulated
PostScript (for commercial printing)

Saving previously saved files

Pull down the File menu and click Save. No dialog launches;
instead, Paint Shop Pro saves the latest version of your file to disk,
overwriting the previous.

Saving copies of images

You can also save a copy of the active picture (and leave the original
intact).

Pull down the File menu and click Save Copy As. Now follow
steps 1–5 above.

Zoom

Paint Shop Pro uses a simple nomenclature to denote what happens when you zoom in or out.

For example, an image at its normal view level is described as:

1:1

If you zoom in three times, this is shown as:

3:1

Alternatively, if you zoom out six times, this is shown as:

1:6

(You can zoom in to 32:1, and out to 1:24.)

You can also use another technique to zoom in. Follow steps 1–2. Now hold down the left mouse button and drag to define the area you want to enlarge. Finally, release the mouse button.

Re step 3 – you should repeat this as often as necessary.

The ability to 'zoom in' (magnify) or 'zoom out' (reduce magnification) is very important when you're working with images in Paint Shop Pro. When you zoom in or out, Paint Shop Pro increases or reduces the magnification by single increments.

1 Click this button in the Tool Palette

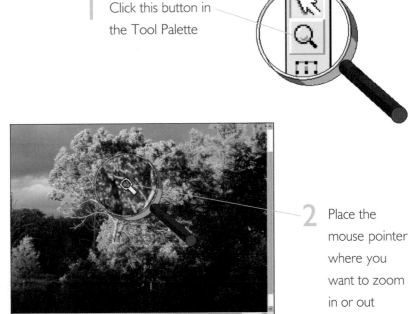

2 Place the mouse pointer where you want to zoom in or out

3 Left-click to zoom in, OR right-click to zoom out

The result of zooming in

The Overview window

When you've zoomed in on part of an image, Paint Shop Pro lets you view the entire image at the same time. You do this by launching the Overview window. This is a very useful feature, though it does have one disadvantage: JASC says it may result in Paint Shop Pro operating more slowly, though we haven't noticed this.

To hide the Overview window, repeat this procedure.

Launching the Overview window

To launch the Overview window, pull down the View menu and click Toolbars. In the dialog, click Overview Window, Close.

Using the Overview window

Do the following:

JASC, the manufacturers of Paint Shop Pro, have their own website. You can use this to:

- *download a free, 30-day trial version of Paint Shop Pro 7*
- *upgrade existing installations of Paint Shop Pro*
- *download update patches to correct problems*
- *download other JASC software. These include WebDraw, the SVG (Scalable Vector Graphics) editor and Namo WebEditor, JASC's professional Web-publishing software*

JASC's Web address is: `http://www.jasc.com`

If an image is being viewed at a high magnification and not all of it displays in its window, the Overview window shows a rectangle representing the visible area. Drag this to view a new area

Full Screen Preview mode

Paint Shop Pro also has another view mode: Full Screen Edit.

This hides:

- *the Title bar*
- *the Menu bar, and;*
- *the Status bar*

To launch (or leave) Full Screen Edit mode, press Shift+A.

Paint Shop Pro has a special screen mode which shows the current image (minus other screen components) set against a black background.

Use Full Screen Preview mode to preview changes you've made (and as a preliminary to running the more detailed Print Preview mode – see Chapter 9).

Entering Full Screen Preview mode

Pull down the View menu and click Full Screen Preview.

An image in Full Edit mode

An image viewed normally

To leave Full Screen Preview, press Esc.

The same image in Full Screen Preview mode

Undo and Revert

You can undo more than one action at a time. Ignore step 1 on the right. Instead, pull down the Edit menu and click Command History. Do the following:

Click an undo level, then click Undo

(Note that selecting a lower undo level automatically selects levels above it).

Paint Shop Pro has two features which, effectively, allow you to revert to the way things were *before* you carried out one or more amendments to the active image.

The Undo command

You can 'undo' (i.e. reverse) the last editing action by issuing a menu command.

Pull down the Edit menu and do the following:

Click Undo ... (the ellipses denote the action being undone)

Repeat step 1 to undo subsequent actions.

The Revert command

You can – in a single command – undo all the editing changes made to an image since it was last saved. You do this by having Paint Shop Pro abandon the changes and reopen the last-saved version of the file.

You can turn off undos if you want. Pull down the File menu and click Preferences, General Program Preferences. Activate the Undo/Redo tab and click Enable the undo system. Click OK.
(Repeat this to reactivate undos.)

Pull down the File menu and click Revert

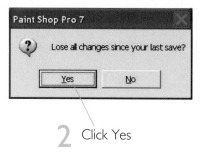

2 Click Yes

Redo

You can redo more than one action at a time. Ignore step 1 on the right. Instead, pull down the Edit menu and click Command History. Do the following:

Paint Shop Pro also lets you undo undoes. This is called 'redoing' an action

The Redo command

You can 'undo' (i.e. reverse) the last editing action by issuing a menu command.

Pull down the Edit menu and do the following:

Click a redo level, then click Redo

Click Redo ... (the ellipses denote the action being redone)

(Clicking a higher redo level automatically selects levels below it).

Redoing in action:

Repeat step 1 to redo subsequent actions.

The Kaleidoscope effect has been applied and then 'undone'...

See Chapter 6 for how to apply effects.

The result of 'redoing' it

Background/foreground colours

Paint Shop Pro uses two broad colour definitions (called 'active' colours):

Foreground colours	These occupy image foregrounds and are invoked with the left mouse button
Background colours	These occupy image backgrounds and are invoked with the right mouse button

If you're working with images with fewer than 16 million colours, Paint Shop Pro 7 only displays 256 colours in the Select Colour panel. This means that when you select a colour, Paint Shop Pro uses that colour which is nearest to the one selected.

(You may find it useful to have the Select Colour panel only display the available 256 colours. To do this, pull down the File menu and click Preferences, General Program Preferences. In the dialog, select the Dialogs and Palettes tab. Activate Show document palette. Click OK.)

The way you work with foreground and background colours is crucial to your use of Paint Shop Pro. Fortunately, selecting the appropriate colours – via the on-screen Colour Palette – is very easy and straightforward.

The Colour Palette defined

The Colour Palette has the following sections:

Document palette display

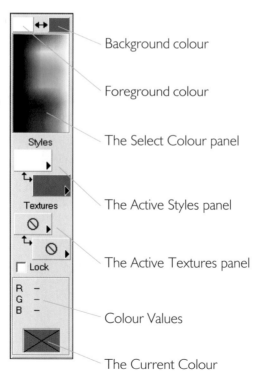

Background colour

Foreground colour

The Select Colour panel

The Active Styles panel

The Active Textures panel

Colour Values

The Current Colour

If you don't want to apply a gradient, texture or pattern in addition to foreground/ background colours, carry out step 1 OR 2. Now click the arrow in the relevant Style or Textures box and click the following icons (respectively) in the fly-out:

 Solid colour

 Null texture

You can make the Colour Palette a freestanding toolbar. Simply drag it onto the screen.
(To return it to the right of the screen, drag it back there.)

The upper Styles and Textures boxes display the foreground stroke/texture, the lower boxes the background fill/ texture.
Use the left mouse button to apply foreground effects, and the right to apply background effects. (This does not apply to the Shape, Text and Line tools.)

Using the Select Colour panel

Move the mouse pointer over any active area in the Select Colour Panel. The pointer changes to:

Move the pointer over the colours in the Select Colour Panel; as you do so, the details in the Current Colour box update automatically. When you find the colour you want to use, do ONE of the following:

1 Left-click once to select it as a foreground colour

2 Right-click once to select it as a background colour

You can now go on to combine the selected foreground or background colours with:

- patterns (called styles)

- gradients (called styles)

- textures

Selecting styles

To select and apply a pattern, follow the relevant procedures on pages 76–77.

To select and apply a gradient, follow steps 1–7 on pages 78–79.

Selecting textures

To select and apply a texture, follow steps 1–7 on pages 80–81.

The Clear command

Paint Shop Pro does not copy the original image or image selection to the Windows Clipboard. If you need to restore the image, however, you can do so by using the Undo feature (see page 22).

You can have Paint Shop Pro automatically replace an image (or a selection within an image) with the current background colour.

Using Clear

1 Set the relevant background colour via the Colour Palette (see pages 24–25)

2 Optional – define the appropriate selection area (see Chapter 2 for how to do this)

3 Pull down the Edit menu and click Clear

Clearing in action:

If you perform steps 1–3 on a floating raster (bitmap) selection, the only effect is to delete the selection.

(On the other hand, steps 1–3 on a vector selection delete the vector object).

See Chapter 2 for more information on selection types.

A selection area has been defined

Clearing a selection area on a layer makes it transparent.

The selection area after a Clear operation

The Product Tour Anniversary Edition only

Paint Shop Pro provides a handy Product Tour which you can use to get help on 7 key program areas. These include:

• Acquiring Images

• Enhancing Photos

• Web Tools

Launching the Product Tour

1 Pull down the Help menu and click Product Tour

2 After a few seconds, a Welcome screen launches. Do the following:

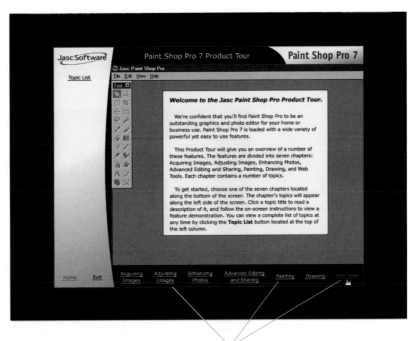

3 Click a topic link

*Re step 4 –
click Next Topic
instead to jump
to the next
topic in the list.*

4 Click Show Me for an
explanatory demonstration

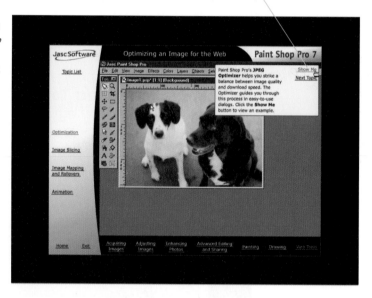

*Choose the
technique you
want help with
here:*

*Click Home to
return to the
Welcome
screen, or Exit
to leave the
Product Tour.*

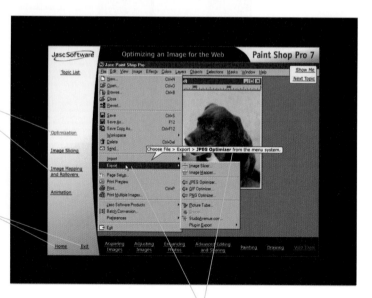

5 Paint Shop Pro leads you
through the selected technique

Using the tutorials Anniversary Edition only

A handy way to supplement your use of this book is provided on the installation CD. You can use a series of tutorials which supply instruction on 10 advanced topics such as:

- Advanced Colour Theory

- Adjusting Skin Tones

- Digital Portrait Techniques

- Creating Your Own Gradients

The tutorials are in .PDF (Adobe Acrobat) format. Acrobat Reader (required to use them) should have been installed along with Paint Shop Pro.

Launching the Tutorials

Pull down the Help menu and click Tutorials

2 Click a topic to jump to it

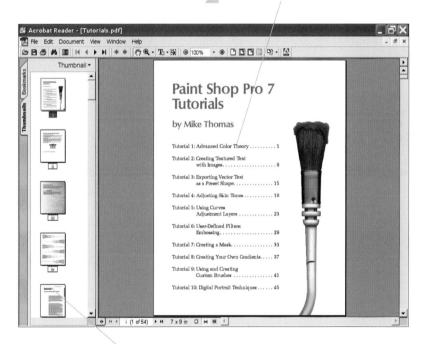

3 Or click a page thumbnail to jump to it

Other ways to move around in the Tutorials

1 Press the Page Down key to move down one page, or the Page Up key to move up by one page

2 Alternatively, perform steps 3–4:

3 Click the Thumbnails tab

4 Click a topic link

For more on how to use Acrobat Reader, see its Help files.

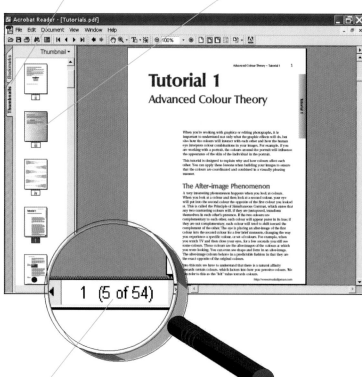

5 Another method: click here. Delete the current details; type in the number of the page you want to go to and press Enter

Making selections

Selecting picture areas is crucial to Paint Shop Pro. Here, you'll learn about selection types. You'll define rectangular, square, elliptical and circular bitmap selections (and even more exotic ones like stars) then select/group previously created vector objects. You'll also deselect, invert and move selections, then amend feathering. Finally, you'll save selections to disk and create multiple/subtractive selections.

Covers

Chapter Two

Selections – an overview

Selecting all or part of a Paint Shop Pro image is the essential preliminary for performing any of the many supported editing operations.

The types on the right are bitmap (raster) selections. However, you can also select vector objects you've created earlier – see page 42.

You can make the following kinds of selections:

- rectangular/square

- elliptical/circular

- triangular

Using combinations of the various types, you can create some truly unique selections.

- hexagonal/octagonal/polygonal

- star-shaped

- arrow-shaped

- freehand

- colour-based

- additive and subtractive

To select the whole of the active image in one go, simply press Ctrl+A. (This also selects vector objects.)

Additionally, you can select an entire image in one operation.

Once part of an image has been selected, you can perform the following, selection-specific operations:

— changing selection modes

— removing (deselecting) selections

— inverting bitmap selections

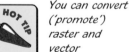

You can convert ('promote') raster and vector selections into raster layers (but note that the part of the new layer not containing the selection is transparent). Simply pull down the Selections menu and click Promote to Layer.

For more information on layers, see Chapter 9.

— moving parts of an image

— amending bitmap feathering (the degree of hardness with which the selection is drawn)

— specifying a transparent colour (as a means of limiting selections)

You can also save image selections to disk as special files (and then reopen them at will within other images) and group/ungroup vector selections.

Selection borders

Selected vector objects (see Chapter 3 for how to create them) have unbroken borders interspersed with nodes e.g.:

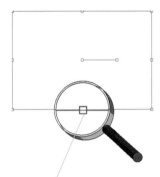

An Edit node – see Chapter 3

There are occasions when it's useful to hide selection marquees – for instance, when you've applied feathering and want to see the result more clearly. Note that hiding marquees does not cancel the selection; it's still there.
To hide the active selection's marquee, pull down the Selections menu and click Hide Marquee. Or press Ctrl+Shift+M.
(Repeat to reverse this.)

Generally, whenever you make a bitmap selection in Paint Shop Pro, you'll select *part* of an image. Whether you do this or select an image in its entirety, the portion you've selected is surrounded with a dotted line:

A magnified view of
the selection border

A rectangular
selection

The selection border (sometimes called a 'marquee') moves, which makes it very easy to locate.

Selection modes

To float a selection, press Ctrl+F. To defloat a selection (return it to Standard), press Ctrl+Shift+F.

You can use two kinds of bitmap selection:

Standard	These form part of the original image. In other words, if you move a selection area (see pages 45–46), Paint Shop Pro fills the resultant gap with the background colour
Floating	When a selection area is floating, the contents are deemed to be on top of (and distinct from) the original

Floating/defloating does not apply to vector objects.

Floating v. Standard selections:

If you float a selection on a vector layer (see Chapter 9 for more information on layers), it is rasterised.

A Standard selection. The selection has been moved, filling the gap with the active background

If you hold down Alt as you drag a Standard selection, it is automatically floated.

A Floating selection. As above, but the underlying image is unaffected

Creating rectangular selections

You can create rectangular bitmap selections in two ways:

- with the use of the mouse
- with the use of a special dialog

If the Tool Options toolbar isn't on-screen, right-click the Tool Palette and select Tool Options in the menu.

The mouse route

Ensure the Tool Palette is on-screen (if it isn't, right-click any toolbar – in the menu, select Tool Palette). Then carry out the following steps:

Re step 2 – if the Tool Options toolbar is on-screen but only its Title bar displays, move the mouse pointer over the Title bar to make the rest of the window appear.

1 Click the Selection tool

To specify the amount of feathering (the sharpness of the selection), type in a value in the Feather: field. Note the following range:

- *0 – maximum sharpness*
- *200 – maximum softness*

2 Refer to the Tool Options toolbar and do the following:

3 Ensure this tab is active

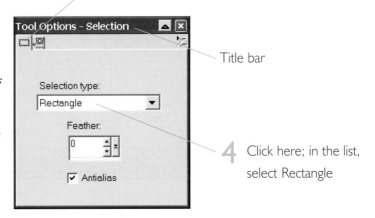

Title bar

Re step 4 – select Rounded Rectangle to round off the corners.

4 Click here; in the list, select Rectangle

Note that the Rectangle and Square selection cursor looks like this:

To create a square selection with the mouse, follow steps 1–3 on page 35. In step 4, select Square (or Rounded Square) instead. Now carry out steps 5–6 on the right.

To create a square selection via a dialog, follow the steps on the right (in step 2, type in the appropriate pixel positions).

Select Surround current selection (if a picture has a prior selection) to surround this. (If the selection is irregular, a rectangular selection is created to encompass it.)

Alternatively, activate one of the 'Opaque' options to isolate and select areas containing data.

5 Place the mouse pointer at the corner of the area you want to select

6 Drag to define the selection

The dialog route

Refer to the Tool Palette and do the following:

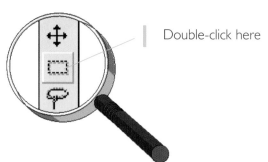

1 Double-click here

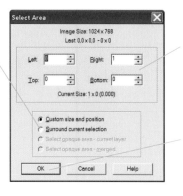

2 Type in the positions (in pixels) of the four corners

3 Click here

Creating elliptical selections

Re step 1 – if the Tool Options toolbar is on-screen but only its Title bar displays, move the mouse pointer over the Title bar to make the rest of the window appear.

1 Perform steps 1–3 on page 35

2 In step 4 on page 35, select Ellipse

3 Place the mouse pointer at the corner of the area you want to select

To create a circular selection, follow step 1 on the right. In step 2, however, select Circle. Now carry out steps 3–4.

To create triangular, hexagonal, octagonal, polygonal, star- or arrow-shaped selections, carry out steps 1–3 on page 35. In step 4, select the appropriate selection type. Finally, position the mouse pointer where you want the selection to start and drag it out.

4 Drag to define the selection

Irregular selections

You can use a special Paint Shop Pro tool – the Freehand tool – to create selections by hand.

Creating freehand selections

Ensure the Tool Palette is on-screen (if it isn't, right-click any toolbar – in the menu, select Tool Palette). Then do the following:

1 Click the Freehand tool

- *Point to Point (the borders are straight), or;*
- *Smart Edge (the borders are defined between contrasting colours/light)*

2 Refer to the Tool Options toolbar and do the following:

3 Ensure this tab is active

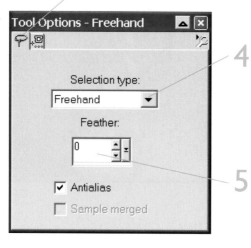

4 Click here; in the list, click Freehand

5 Type in a Feathering setting (in the range: 0–200)

The Freehand cursor looks like this:

6 Place the mouse pointer at the location where you want the selection to begin

7 Drag to define the selection

You can contract or expand bitmap selections uniformly (the shape is retained) via a dialog.

Pull down the Selections menu and click Modify, Contract or Modify, Expand. In the Number of pixels: field in the dialog which launches, type in the extent of the contraction or expansion (in pixels). Click OK.

You can also expand a selection (but only in images with 16 million colours or more) to include contiguous and similar colours.

Pull down the Selections menu and click Modify, Grow Selection.

(Note that this feature uses the Magic Wand tool settings – see steps 3–4 on page 40.)

Selections based on colour

If the Tool Options toolbar isn't on-screen, right-click the Tool Palette and select Tool Options in the menu.

You can use another Paint Shop Pro tool – the Magic Wand – to select portions of the active image which share a specific colour.

Creating colour-based selections

Ensure the Tool Palette is on-screen (if it isn't, right-click any toolbar – in the menu, select Tool Palette). Then do the following:

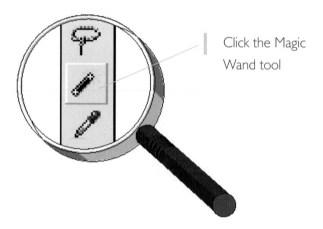

Click the Magic
Wand tool

Type in a value in the Tolerance field. (Tolerance is the degree to which image pixels must approach the chosen one to activate selection.) Use this range:

- *0 – only exact matches result in selection*
- *200 – all pixels are selected*

2 Refer to the Tool Options toolbar and do the following:

3 Ensure this tab is active

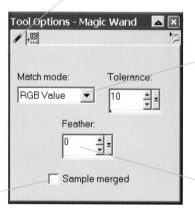

4 Click here; in the list, click a selection method

Tick Sample merged to make a selection based on all (not just the active) layers.

5 Type in a Feathering setting (in the range: 0–200)

The Magic Wand cursor looks like this:

You can expand a selection (but only in images with 16 million colours or more, or in greyscale images) to include non-contiguous and similar colours. Pull down the Selections menu and click Modify, Select Similar.

(Note that this feature uses the Magic Wand tool settings – see steps 3–4 on the facing page.)

You can also expand a selection to include similar colours which are contiguous. Pull down the Selections menu and click Modify, Grow Selection.

(The provisos listed in the HOT TIP above also apply to this procedure.)

To remove a specific colour from an existing selection, follow steps 1–5 on the facing page. Now hold down Ctrl as you click the colour.

6 Place the mouse pointer over the area you want to select and left-click once

7 The new selection area

Vector selections

To select vector objects you've already created, carry out the following procedure.

Selecting one vector object

See chapter 3 for how to create vector objects.

To deselect all selections you've already made, pull down the Selections menu and click Select None.

Alternatively, if the Selection, Freehand or Magic Wand tools are active, right-click once outside the selection(s).

To specifically deselect all vector selections, press Ctrl+D.

Refer to the Tool Palette and do the following:

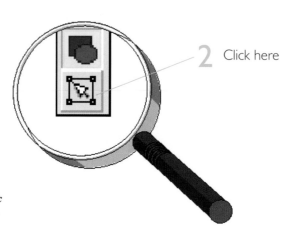

2 Click here

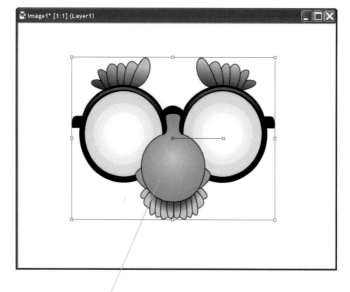

3 Click a vector object (or its outline)

Selecting multiple vector objects

1 Carry out steps 1–2 on the facing page

You can also use another technique to select more than one vector object. Follow step 1 then hold down Shift as you click them.

You can also use the Layer palette to select vector objects. Launch the Layer palette by right-clicking any toolbar and selecting Layer Palette. Then do the following:

Hold down Shift and click each object's layer name button

2 Drag out a marquee around the objects you want to select, then release the mouse button

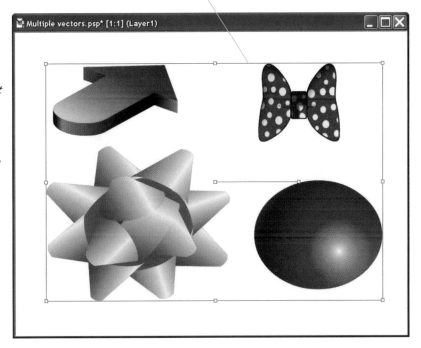

3 Alternatively, hold down Shift as you left-click on successive objects

4 To remove a vector object from a selection group, hold down Ctrl as you left-click it

Inverting selections

When you've selected a portion of an image, you can have Paint Shop Pro do BOTH of the following:

- deselect the selected area

- select the external area which was previously unselected

Paint Shop Pro calls this 'inverting a selection'. Use inversion as a means of creating selections which would otherwise be difficult – or impossible – to achieve.

Inverting a selection

First make a normal selection. Then pull down the Selections menu and click Invert.

Inversion in action:

In the lower figure, Paint Shop Pro has also surrounded the selected area (here, the image minus the additive selection) with a dotted border:

An additive selection (see page 51)

After inversion – the marquee now encloses the *unselected* area

Moving selections

Paint Shop Pro lets you move bitmap selections (by detaching them from the host layer). You can:

- move just the frame which defines the selection area

OR

- move the frame AND the contents

To move a vector object, ensure this Tool Palette tool is active:

Now click the object's outline (not its bounding box). Keep the pointer on the outline until it becomes a four-pronged arrow. Hold down the left mouse button and drag the object to a new location.

You can also use the Mover tool to move frames AND contents.
First, ensure the selection is floating (if it isn't, press Ctrl+F). Finally, carry out steps 2–4.

Moving selection frames only

1   Ensure the selection you want to move isn't floating (if it is, press Ctrl+Shift+F)

2   Refer to the Tool Palette and do the following:

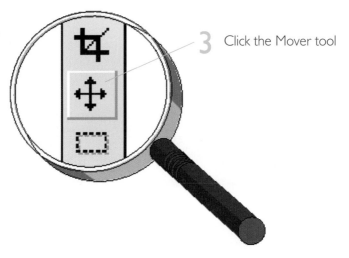

3   Click the Mover tool

4   Right-click inside the existing selection area, then drag it to a new location

You can also move selections and their contents with the keyboard.

Hold down Shift. Now press and hold down any of the cursor keys.

(Hold down Ctrl as well as Shift to increase the move speed.)

Moving bitmap selection frames and contents

First, ensure that the selection area is Standard or Floating, according to the effect you want to achieve. (See page 34 for a description of the two possible effects). Then:

1   In the Tool Palette, activate the tool which was used to create the selection

2   Drag the selection to a new location

The procedures in the above tip also apply to selected vector objects (except that the underlying image is unaffected).

Moving selection contents in action:

When you move a Standard selection, the original area is filled with the active background colour.

Moving the contents of a Standard selection

An advanced user's tip – hold down Ctrl and Alt while pressing any of the arrow keys to:

- *copy the selection (leaving the original unaffected)*
- *move it one pixel at a time*

simultaneously.

Moving the contents of a Floating selection

Amending selection feathering

Re step 1 – feathering is the sharpness of the selection. Note the range:

- *0 – maximum sharpness*
- *200 – maximum softness*

As we've seen, when you define a selection within an image, you have the opportunity to customise the feathering. However, you can also do this (and to a greater extent) *after* the selection area has been created.

Imposing a new feathering

Define a selection. Pull down the Selections menu and click Modify, Feather. Now do the following:

Moving selections (see pages 45–46) leaves some of the surrounding pixels attached to the selection border:

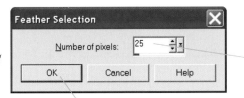

Type in a new feathering

2 Click here

Unwanted pixels

A magnified view of the feathered selection edge

The pixels have been removed

To correct this, ensure the selection is floating. Click Selections, Matting. Then click Defringe, Remove White Matte or Remove Black Matte, as appropriate.

This square selection has been dragged to the right

Selecting a transparent colour

The Remove Selected Colour dialog only lets you select a few basic colours.

For more precision, though, follow the procedures on page 25 to select a specific background or foreground colour, then select Foreground Colour or Background Colour in step 1. Finally, follow step 2.

You can specify a transparent colour; this tells Paint Shop Pro to deselect it within a selection.

Selecting a colour

Define a selection. Pull down the Selections menu and click Modify, Transparent Colour. Now do the following:

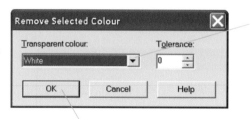

1 Click here; in the list, select a colour

2 Click here

Also type in a value in the Tolerance field. (Tolerance is the degree to which image pixels must approach the chosen one to activate selection.) Use this range:

- *0 – only exact matches result in selection*

- *200 – all pixels are selected*

Transparent colour selection in action:

Moving this selection area illustrates transparent colour selection – see the DON'T FORGET tip

In this example, a rectangular selection was made around the turret, then one of the turret colours was selected as the Foreground colour (with a fairly low tolerance) using the technique discussed in the HOT TIP at the top of the page. In step 1, Foreground Colour was selected. Then, when the frame was moved to the left, all colours apart from the foreground were moved.

Reusing selections

Paint Shop Pro lets you save a selection area (the frame, NOT the contents) to disk, as a special file. You can then load it into a new image. This is a convenient way to reuse complex selections.

An unusual selection, saved to disk...

 See pages 51–52 for how to create selections like this.

... and then loaded into another image

Selection files have the suffix: .SEL

Saving a selection

Define a selection. Pull down the Selections menu and click Save To Disk. Now do the following:

Click here; in the drop-down

list, select a drive

Re step 1 – you may also have to double-click one or more folders first, to locate the folder you want to save the selection to.

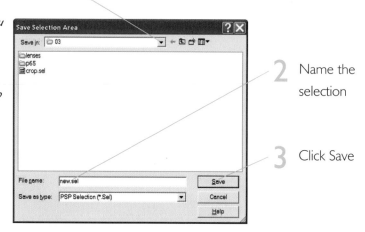

2 Name the selection

3 Click Save

Loading a selection

Pull down the Selections menu and click Load From Disk. Now do the following:

Re step 1 – you may also have to double-click one or more folders first, to locate the folder which hosts the relevant selection file.

Click here; in the drop-down

list, select a drive

2 Double-click a selection

Selection additions/subtractions

HOT TIP When you create multiple selections, a plus sign is added to the cursor for the relevant tool. For example, the Rectangle selector looks like this:

You can define multiple (additive) selections. This is a very useful technique which enables you to create spectacular effects. You can also create selections subtractively, where Paint Shop Pro decreases the size of a selection in line with further contiguous selections you define.

Creating multiple (additive) selections

1 Define the first selection, using any of the techniques previously discussed:

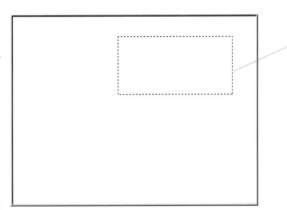

Here, a rectangular selection has been created

HOT TIP Re step 2 – if (as here) you define a further selection which encroaches onto the first, the two are joined. If, on the other hand, you define the second selection so that it does not touch the first, this creates two separate selections:

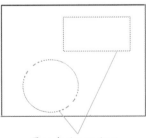

Two independent selections

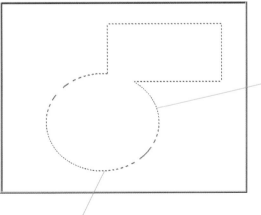

A further elliptical selection has been defined (forming one unusual selection)

DON'T FORGET Re step 2 – if you're using the Magic Wand to create multiple selections, simply hold down Shift as you click the area you want to add.

2 Hold down Shift, then define another selection

Creating subtractive selections

1 Define the first selection, using any of the techniques previously discussed:

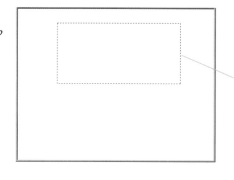

When you perform selection subtractions, Paint Shop Pro adds a minus sign to the cursor for the relevant selection tool. For example, the Rectangle selector looks like this:

Here, a rectangular selection has been created

Re step 2 – if you're using the Magic Wand tool, simply hold down Ctrl as you click within the first selection area – Paint Shop Pro subtracts the second selection from the first.

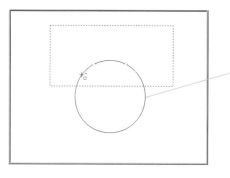

2 Hold down Ctrl as you define another contiguous selection

3 Release the mouse button

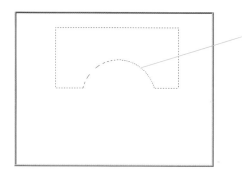

Paint Shop Pro has 'subtracted' the second selection from the first

Grouping/ungrouping

Paint Shop Pro lets you organise vector objects into 'groups'. When grouped, objects can be manipulated jointly in the normal way (for instance, you can save/load them.)

Grouping vector objects

Grouping vectors automatically moves them to the same layer.

1 First select all the relevant vector objects (see page 43 for how to do this)

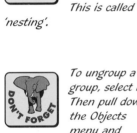

You can have groups within groups (up to 100 levels). This is called 'nesting'.

2 Pull down the Objects menu and click Group

To ungroup a group, select it. Then pull down the Objects menu and select UnGroup.

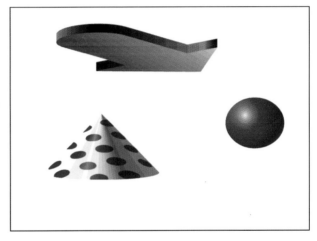

Ungrouped vector objects

Here, all three objects were selected by clicking just one with the Object Selector tool active:

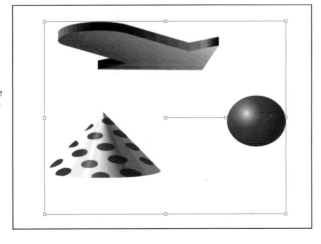

Grouped vector objects

Removing grouped vector objects

You can remove single objects from groups.

I If the Layer palette isn't on screen, right click any toolbar. In the menu, click Layer palette

4 Drag the vector to a new layer (as here) or group

If necessary, first click the plus sign here: to display all layers.

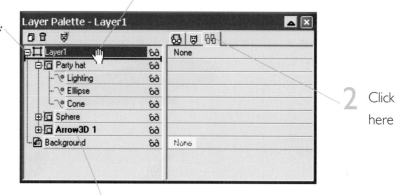

2 Click here

3 Click a group member

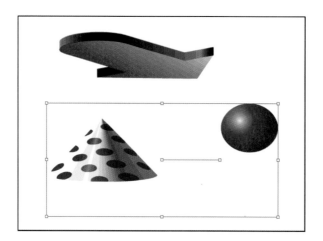

Now, the arrow is no longer part of the group

Painting and drawing

In this chapter, you'll use a variety of techniques, many of which can be employed with scanned-in images or photographs captured via digital cameras. You'll perform freehand painting; copy colours; carry out colour substitutions; select specific colours for foreground/background use; retouch images; spray-paint; fill images with colours, patterns, other images, gradients and textures; and paint with object collections (picture tubes).

Finally, you'll format and insert text; create lines and preset shapes (including saving them to a library for future use); then reshape them by moving their nodes.

Covers

Chapter Three

Painting/drawing – an overview

Paint Shop Pro lets you paint and draw on-screen, using a variety of specialised but easy to use tools located within the Tools Palette.

You can:

With many of the operations in this chapter, you can restrict the effect to specific image parts by using selection areas or masks.

- create freehand paintings/drawings

- copy colours within images

- carry out colour substitutions (globally and manually)

- carry out image retouching (the manual application of special effects to images or image selections)

- carry out spray painting/drawing

- fill images with colours

- fill images with patterns (or other images)

- fill images with textures

- fill images with gradients

- insert raster or vector text into images

- edit/format existing vector text

- apply vector text onto vector object outlines

- create single, freehand and Bézier lines/curves

- create preset shapes (circles, ellipses, squares, rectangles, triangles or more complex shapes)

- save vectors you create to a 'library', for future use

- paint with object collections (called 'picture tubes')

- reshape vector objects by manipulating their nodes (you can also create your own), handles and contours

Painting with the Paintbrush tool

Re step 4 – you should make use of the following guidelines:

- *Shape – select a shape (e.g. Square or Horizontal)*

- *Size – select a brush size in pixels (in the range 1– 255)*

- *Hardness – select a % in the range 0–100*

- *Opacity – select a % in the range 1–100 (100 is maximum opacity)*

- *Step (mimics brush contact) – select a % in the range 1–100*

- *Density – select a % in the range 1–100*

Creating a painting

Refer to the Tool palette and do the following:

1 Click here

2 Refer to the Tool Options toolbar and do the following:

3 Ensure this tab is active

4 Complete these fields

5 Place the mouse pointer where you want to start painting

Re step 6 – you should carry out one of the following operations:

- *drag with the left mouse button to paint with the active foreground colour/ style/texture (see page 25), or;*

- *drag with the right mouse button to paint with the active background colour/ style/texture*

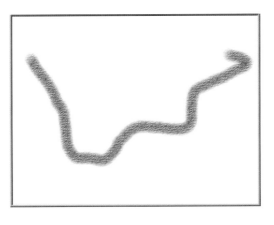

6 Define the painting, then release the mouse button

Drawing with the Paintbrush tool

Drawing lines

Refer to the Tool palette and do the following:

| Click here

You can also use the Draw tool to draw lines – see pages 86–88.

2 Complete steps 2–4 on page 57

3 Click where you want the first line segment to begin

Right-click if you want to draw with the background colour/style/ texture.

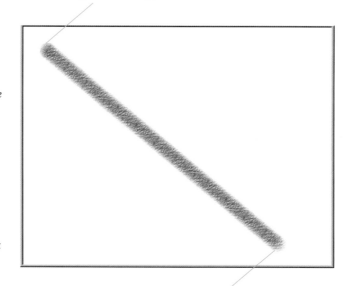

Repeat step 4 to define any further line segments which are required.

4 Hold down Shift, then click where you want the first segment to end

Copying with the Clone brush

Cloning is the copying of colour from one location within an image to another (or to another image which has the same number of colours). To clone colours, you use the Clone brush.

Cloning
Refer to the Tool palette and do the following:

Click here

Re step 4 – you should use the following notes as guidelines:

- *Shape – select a shape (e.g. Square or Horizontal)*

- *Size – select a brush size in pixels (in the range 1–255)*

- *Hardness – select a % in the range 0–100*

- *Opacity – select a % in the range 1–100 (100 = maximum opacity)*

- *Step (mimics brush contact) – select a % in the range 1–100*

- *Density – select a % in the range 1–100*

2 Refer to the Tool Options toolbar and do the following:

3 Ensure this tab is active

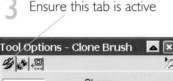

4 Complete the dialog's fields, as appropriate

5 Carry out the additional steps overleaf

6 Place the mouse pointer over the image section you want to copy

7 Right-click once

The Clone crosshairs indicate the pixel which is currently being copied.

As you drag in step 8, the crosshairs move, so you can select (on-the-fly) the area being copied.

8 Position the cursor where you want the paste operation to take place, then drag repeatedly

Magnified view of crosshairs

Replacing colours globally

You can have Paint Shop Pro replace a specified colour with another. You do this by nominating the colour you want to replace as the foreground colour, then selecting the new colour as the background colour. (Or vice versa).

You can replace colours:

- globally (within the whole of an image, or a selection area)

- manually (by using the Colour Replacer tool as a brush)

Re step 4 – you should use the following notes as guidelines:

- *Shape – select a shape (e.g. Square or Horizontal)*

- *Size – select a brush size in pixels (in the range 1– 255)*

- *Step (mimics brush contact) – select a % in the range 1–100*

- *Density – select a % in the range 1–100*

Carrying out a global substitution

Refer to the Tool palette and do the following:

1 Click here

2 Refer to the Tool Options toolbar and do the following:

3 Ensure this tab is active

This dialog is slightly different in the non-Anniversary edition of Paint Shop Pro.

4 Complete the dialog's fields, as appropriate

5 Carry out the additional steps overleaf

6 Optional – if you want to limit the colour exchange to a selected area, define the relevant area now

7 Carry out step 8 OR 9 below:

8 Double-click the left mouse button to replace the background with the foreground colour

9 Double-click the right mouse button to replace the foreground with the background colour

The end result:

Here, the colour in the saucer (and part of the cup) has been replaced with white...

Replacing colours manually

Carrying out a manual substitution

Refer to the Tool palette and do the following:

Replacing colours manually requires a light touch (and experimentation with the available settings – see step 2).

Click here

Re step 3 – you should carry out ONE of the following procedures:

- *drag with the left mouse button to replace the background with the foreground colour, or;*
- *drag with the right mouse button to replace the foreground with the background colour*

2 Complete steps 2–4 on page 61

3 Drag over the relevant area to carry out the substitution – see the DON'T FORGET tip

4 Release the mouse button when you've finished

Replacing colours with lines

Replacing colours with lines requires a light touch (and experimentation with the available settings).

The Colour Replacer tool also lets you substitute colours as you create lines.

Replacing colours while drawing lines

Refer to the Tool palette and do the following:

Click here

Re steps 3–4 – you should carry out one of the following procedures:

- *click with the left mouse button to replace the background with the foreground colour, or;*
- *click with the right mouse button to replace the foreground with the background colour*

2 Complete steps 2–4 on page 61

3 Click where you want the line to start

Here, the roof is being replaced with white.

Repeat step 4 as often as necessary.

4 To create a line segment, hold down Shift and click elsewhere

Using the Dropper tool

You can activate the Dropper within most paint tools by holding down Ctrl.

The Dropper is an extremely useful tool which you can use to:

1. select a colour in the active image

2. nominate this as the active foreground or background colour

Using the Dropper

Refer to the Tool palette and do the following:

Re step 2 – you should carry out one of the following procedures:

*   *click with the left mouse button to nominate the selected colour as the foreground, or;*

*   *click with the right mouse button to nominate the selected colour as the background*

Click here

After step 2, the selected colour appears in the Colour Palette:

Selected colours

Here, the fly-out indicates (using the RGB colour scheme) that the colour selected is white.

The makeup of the colour selected in step 2 displays in a fly-out:

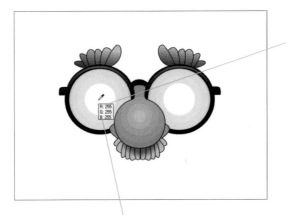

R: 255
G: 255
B: 255

2 Click a colour – see the DON'T FORGET tip

Retouching – an overview

You can use the Retouch tool to perform photo-retouching operations on images (or selected areas). These operations include:

Lighten RGB	Makes the image or selection brighter
Darken RGB	Makes the image or selection darker
Soften	Mutes the image or selection and diminishes contrast
Sharpen	Emphasises edges and accentuates contrast
Emboss	Produces a raised ('stamped') effect (where the foreground is emphasised in relation to the background)
Smudge	Produces a stained, blurred effect
Push	Like Smudge but no colour is picked up
Dodge	Lightens image shadow
Burn	Darkens images

All the above tools (excluding Dodge and Burn) work with images which are 24 bit (16 million colours) or greyscale; the remainder work only with 24 bit images.

Ways to use the Retouch tool

You can use the Retouch tool:

– as a brush

– to draw lines

Retouching images manually

Retouching images manually requires a light touch (and experimentation with the available settings – see step 2).

After step 2, to select a retouch operation Anniversary edition users should click in the Mode field (untitled) at the base of the Tool Options toolbar. In the list, select an operation.

Users of the non-Anniversary edition should first click this tab in the toolbar instead:

Now they should click in the Retouch mode: field and select an operation in the list.

For information on how to include patterns, textures or gradients in operations you perform with the Retouch tool, see page 25.

Here, an Emboss retouching operation is being carried out.

Carrying out a manual retouch operation

Refer to the Tool palette and do the following:

Click here

2 Complete steps 2–4 on page 68, as appropriate

3 Hold down the left mouse button and drag over the relevant area

4 Release the mouse button when you've finished

Retouching images with lines

To retouch images by defining lines, carry out the procedures described below.

Retouching images while drawing lines

Refer to the Tool palette and do the following:

Click here

Re step 4 – for how to complete these fields, see the HOT TIP on page 61.

2 Refer to the Tool Options toolbar and do the following:

3 Ensure this tab is active

Anniversary edition users should click in this field. In the list, select a retouch operation.

Users of the non-Anniversary edition should follow a different procedure. First click this tab in the toolbar:

Now click in the Retouch mode: field and select an operation in the list.

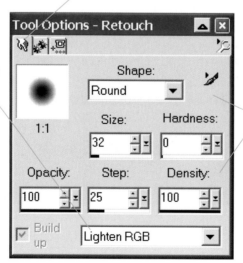

4 Complete these fields, as appropriate (this dialog looks slightly different in the non-Anniversary edition – see the HOT TIP)

5 Click where you want the
retouch operation to begin

*For information
on how to
include
patterns,
textures or
gradients in operations you
perform with the Retouch
tool, see page 25.*

*Here, a Burn
retouching
operation is
being carried
out.*

*Repeat step 6
for as many
extra line
segments as
you want to
insert.*

6 Hold down Shift and click where you
want the line segment to end

Painting with the Airbrush

You can use the Airbrush tool to simulate painting with a spray can. You can do this in two ways:

* while using the Airbrush as a brush

* while using the Airbrush to draw lines

Using the Airbrush as a brush

Refer to the Tool palette and do the following:

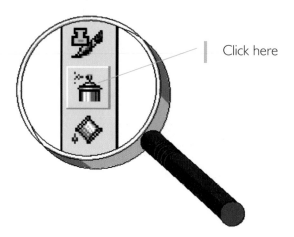

Click here

You can also select and apply a brush type.
After step 3, click this button on the right of the Tool Options toolbar:

In the menu, select a brush (e.g. Paintbrush or Charcoal).
(Alternatively, click Custom in the menu. In the Custom Brush dialog, click a brush. Finally, click OK.)

2 Refer to the Tool Options toolbar and do the following:

3 Ensure this tab is active

4 Complete these fields, as appropriate (see the HOT TIP on page 57)

5 Carry out step 6 OR 7 below:

6 Hold down the left mouse button, then drag to paint with the active foreground colour/style/texture

Here, the Shape setting (see step 4 on the facing page) has been set to Left Slash.

For information on how to include patterns, textures or gradients in operations you perform with the Airbrush tool, see page 25.

7 Hold down the right mouse button, then drag to paint with the active background colour/ style/texture

8 Release the mouse button

Drawing with the Airbrush

Using the Airbrush to draw lines

Refer to the Tool palette and do the following:

You can also select and apply a brush type.
After step 3, click this button on the right of the Tool Options toolbar:

In the menu, select a brush (e.g. Paintbrush or Charcoal).
(Alternatively, click Custom in the menu. In the Custom Brush dialog, click a brush. Finally, click OK.)

Click here

2 Refer to the Tool Options toolbar and do the following:

3 Ensure this tab is active

4 Complete the dialog's fields, as appropriate (see the HOT TIP on page 57)

... cont'd

5 Click where you want the
retouch operation to begin

For information
on how to
include
patterns,
textures or
gradients in operations you
perform with the Airbrush
tool, see page 25.

Here, a custom
brush has been
applied – see
the HOT TIP on
the facing page.

Repeat step 6
for as many
extra line
segments as
you want to
insert.

6 Hold down Shift and click where you
want the line segment to end

Inserting colours with the Fill tool

You can use the Fill tool to

- fill an image with colour

- fill an image with a specific image you've already opened into an additional window

- fill an image with a gradient (Paint Shop Pro supports 4 kinds: Linear, Rectangular, Sunburst, Radial)

Filling images with a colour

Refer to the Tool palette and do the following:

If you want to limit the fill to a selection area, define it before step 1.

Click here

Re step 4 – you should use the following notes as guidelines:

- *Blend mode – all options except Normal ensure that the fill is affected by the underlying image colours*

- *Match mode – select the method by which Paint Shop Pro decides which pixels are covered (None covers all pixels)*

- *Opacity – select a % in the range 1–100 (100 is maximum opacity), and;*

- *Tolerance – enter a value in this range: 0 (only exact matches are filled) to 200 (every pixel is filled)*

2 Refer to the Tool Options toolbar and do the following:

3 Ensure this tab is active

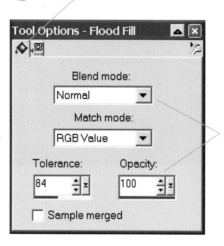

4 Complete the dialog's fields, as appropriate

5 Left-click to insert the foreground colour, OR right-click to insert the background colour

For information on how to include patterns, textures or gradients in operations you perform with the Fill tool, see page 25.

A completed colour fill:

Inserting images as patterns

You can use the Colour Palette to apply images as patterns to other images.

Filling an image with another

First, open:

1.   the image you want to insert

2.   the image into which you want to insert it

Now refer to the Colour Palette and do the following:

The procedure as set out here applies the selected image as a foreground pattern. To apply it as a background pattern instead, note that steps 1–3 should refer to the lower Styles button instead of the upper one.

To insert a preset pattern into images as a foreground fill, follow steps 1–4. In step 5, however, select a pre-defined pattern (e.g. Blue Strings) rather than another image.

(To insert a preset pattern as a background fill, note that steps 1–3 should refer to the lower Styles button instead of the upper one.)

Finally, carry out step 6.

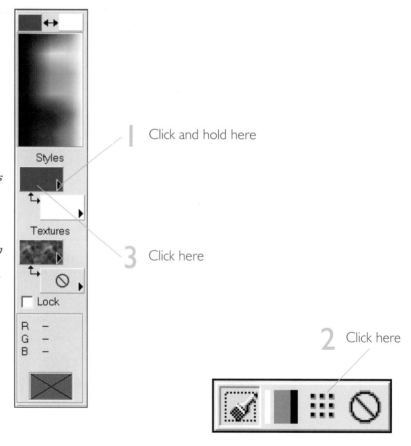

4 Click here

Note that the images you apply pattern fills to must be at least:

- *24 bit (16 million colours), or;*
- *greyscale*

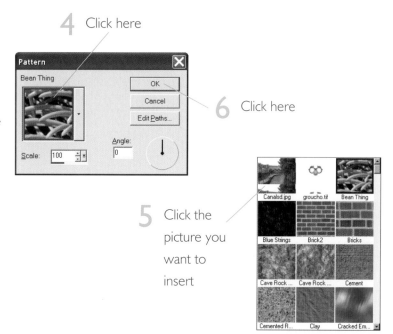

6 Click here

5 Click the picture you want to insert

7 Follow steps 1–4 on page 74, then left-click in the host image to insert the picture/pattern

Two images combined in an unusual way:

Inserting gradients

You can use the Colour Palette to apply gradients to images.

Filling images with a gradient

First, open the image you want to fill (or pre-define a selection area). Now refer to the Colour Palette and do the following:

Rectangular

Sunburst

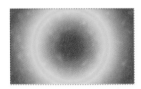

Radial

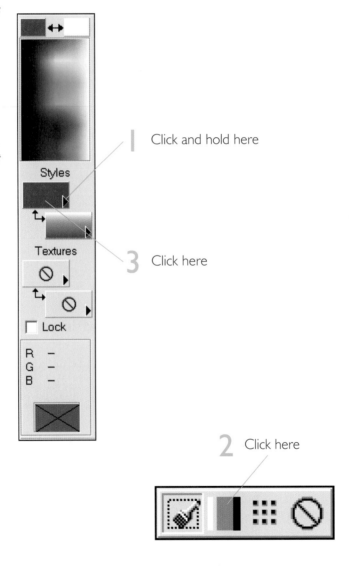

1 Click and hold here

3 Click here

2 Click here

Before you carry out step 6, select a gradient type on the right of the dialog.

The topmost icon creates a linear gradient. For details of the other icons, see the HOT TIP on the facing page.

4 Click here

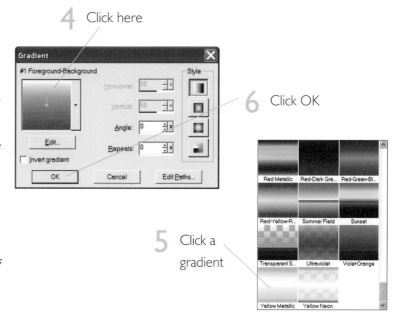

6 Click OK

5 Click a gradient

Note that the images you apply gradients to must be at least:

- *24 bit (16 million colours), or;*
- *greyscale*

7 Follow steps 1–4 on page 74, then left-click in the image to insert the gradient

Additional tools with which you can apply gradients include the following:

- *Paintbrush*
- *Clone*
- *Colour Replacer*
- *Retouch*
- *Airbrush*

A radial gradient applied to a bitmap:

Inserting textures

You can use the Colour Palette to apply gradients to images.

Filling images with a texture

First, open the image you want to fill (or pre-define a selection area). Now refer to the Colour Palette and do the following:

The procedures described here insert a texture in the foreground. To insert one as a background fill, note that steps 1 and 3 should refer to the lower Textures button instead.

You can only apply textures in conjunction with active foreground or background styles.

(In the illustration on the facing page, the texture has been applied with a solid fill.)

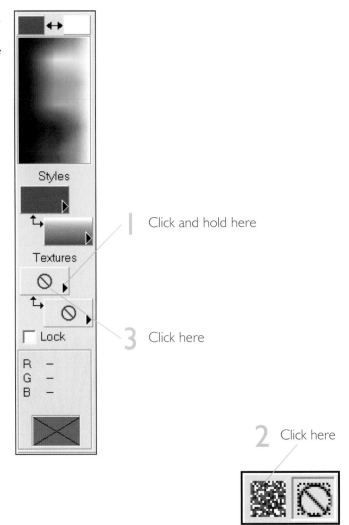

Click and hold here

3 Click here

2 Click here

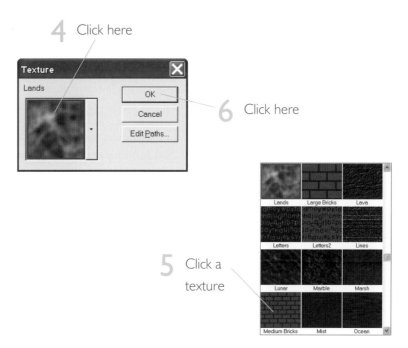

4 Click here

6 Click here

5 Click a texture

Note that the images you apply textures to must be at least:

- 24 bit (16 million colours), or;
- greyscale

Additional tools with which you can apply gradients include the following:

- Paintbrush
- Clone
- Colour Replacer
- Retouch
- Airbrush

7 Follow steps 1–4 on page 74, then left-click in the image to insert the gradient

A texture applied to a bitmap:

Inserting text with the Text tool

Paint Shop Pro lets you insert text into images, easily and conveniently. You can insert two principal types of text:

Once created, Selection text can be edited with Paint Shop Pro's tools. In the following example, a different gradient fill has been applied to each letter:

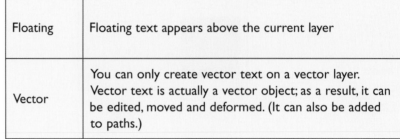

Floating	Floating text appears above the current layer
Vector	You can only create vector text on a vector layer. Vector text is actually a vector object; as a result, it can be edited, moved and deformed. (It can also be added to paths.)

When you create text, you can specify:

1. a typeface and/or type size

2. a style. With most typefaces, you can choose from:

    Regular

    – *Italic*

    – **Bold**

3. the following text effects

    – ~~Strikethrough~~

    – Underline

4. an alignment. You can choose from:

    – Left

    –   Center

    –   Right

You can also elect to have Paint Shop Pro 'anti-alias' the text.

You can insert vector text onto simple vector object outlines.
With the Text tool active in the Tool palette, move the mouse pointer over the relevant vector object until the cursor changes:

The new cursor

Now click the vector object. Complete the Text Entry dialog in line with steps 4–9 overleaf (ensure Vector is selected in step 6, and make sure you select the appropriate alignment in step 7).

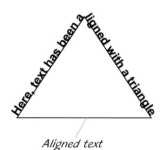

Aligned text

Inserting text

Refer to the Tool palette and do the following:

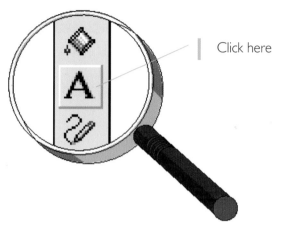

1 Click here

2 Place the mouse pointer where you want the text inserted

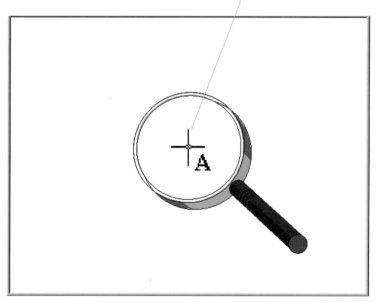

3 Left-click once

You can insert vector text onto open vector paths (open paths have start and end points).

With the Text tool active in the Tool palette, move the mouse pointer over the relevant vector path until the cursor changes:

4 Click here; in the list, select a font

5 Click here; in the list, select a type size

7 Click 1 or more formatting options

9 Click OK

6 Select a text type

8 Type in your text

The new cursor

Text in action:

Now click the path. Complete the Text Entry dialog in line with steps 4–9 (ensure Vector is selected in step 6, and make sure you select the appropriate alignment in step 7).

Aligned text

Editing text

Paint Shop Pro lets you edit inserted vector text. Do the following:

1 Click here in the Tool palette

2 Place the mouse pointer over the text and left-click – the Text Entry dialog launches

3 Carry out steps 4–7 (as appropriate) on the facing page

4 Carry out step 8 on the facing page (but amend the existing text as appropriate)

5 Carry out step 9 on the facing page

Drawing with the Draw tool

After step 1, click this tab in the Tool Options toolbar:

Now click in the Type: field. In the list, select Single Line. Also, click in the Line style: field and select a style in the list – e.g., you can select a dotted line, or one with arrowheads on one or both ends.

Finally, enter a line width in the Width: field (in the range 1–255) and select Create as vector (for a fully editable line).

For information on how to include patterns, textures or gradients in operations you perform with the Draw tool, see page 25.

Paint Shop Pro has a separate tool which you can use to create more detailed lines/curves.

You can draw:

- Single lines

- Freehand lines

- Bézier curves

You can create lines/curves as rasters or vectors (as ever, vectors are much more editable).

Drawing single lines

Refer to the Tool palette and do the following:

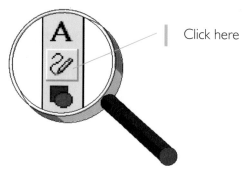

Click here

2 Place the mouse pointer where you want the line to start

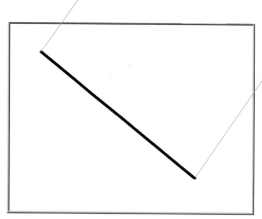

3 Drag with the left mouse button to draw the line

Drawing single lines with multiple segments

Refer to the Tool palette and do the following:

1 Follow step 1 on the facing page

2 Place the mouse pointer where you want the line to start, then left-click once

3 Hold down Alt

4 Click where you want the segment to end, and click again

5 Repeat for as many segments as you want to add, still holding down Alt

6 Release Alt and click for the last time

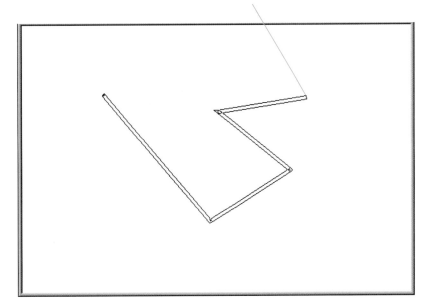

7 Paint Shop Pro fills out the line outline

For information on how to include patterns, textures or gradients in operations you perform with the Draw tool, see page 25.

Drawing Freehand lines

Refer to the Tool palette and do the following:

1 Follow step 1 on page 86

2 Refer to the Tool Options toolbar and do the following:

3 Ensure this tab is active

Select Create as vector to define a vector Freehand line, or deselect this to create a raster line.

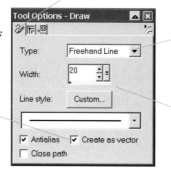

4 Click here; in the list, select Freehand Line

5 Complete the remaining fields, as appropriate

6 Drag with the left mouse button to draw with the foreground colour, or with the right to draw with the background colour

Here, a vector Freehand line has been defined.

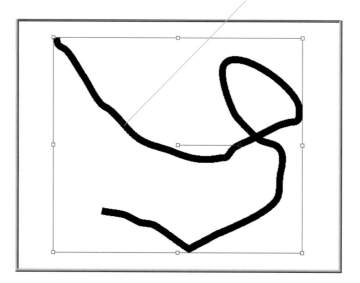

Drawing Bézier curves

Refer to the Tool palette and do the following:

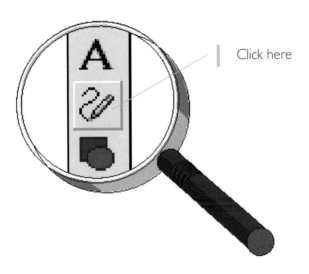

1   Click here

2   Refer to the Tool Options toolbar and do the following:

3   Ensure this tab is active

Select Create as vector to define a vector Freehand line, or deselect this to create a raster line.

Tool Options - Draw

Type: Bezier Curve

Width: 20

Line style: Custom...

☑ Antialias   ☑ Create as vector
☐ Close path

4   Click here; in the list, select Bézier Curve

5   Complete the remaining fields, as appropriate

6   Carry out the additional steps overleaf

7 Place the mouse pointer where you want the curve to start

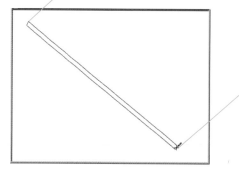

8 Drag with the left mouse button to define the curve's length

9 Click away from the start point to set the start target angle

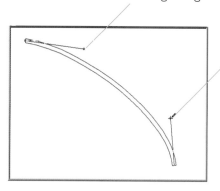

10 Click away from the end point to set the end target angle

The end result:

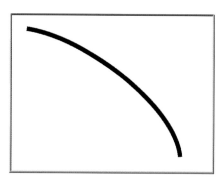

Here, a raster curve has been defined

Using the Picture Tube tool

You can also paint using object collections called 'picture tubes'. When you do this, Paint Shop Pro automatically inserts a variety of related objects. For instance, if you paint with the Fish picture tube, a dozen different fish types are inserted...

Painting with the Picture Tube tool

Refer to the Tool palette and do the following:

1 Click here

2 Refer to the Tool Options toolbar and do the following:

Re step 5 – complete the fields in line with the following guidelines:

- *Scale – set the tube size (in the range 10%–250%)*

- *Step – increase the step setting to give less contact between the brush tip and the image surface. The result is that the tube's outline is more prominent, and the stroke less dense*

3 Ensure this tab is active

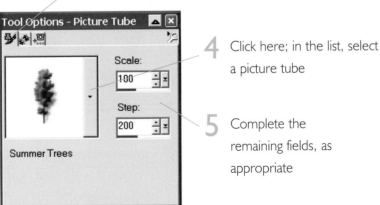

4 Click here; in the list, select a picture tube

5 Complete the remaining fields, as appropriate

6 Carry out the additional steps overleaf

7 Ensure this tab is active

*Re step 8 –
complete the
fields in line
with the
following
guidelines:*

- *Placement mode – select
Random (objects appear
at random intervals) or
Continuous (objects are
inserted at equal
intervals), and;*

- *Selection mode – select
Random (objects are
chosen haphazardly);
Incremental (objects are
inserted one at a time);
Angular (objects appear
according to painting
direction); or Velocity
(objects appear according
to painting speed)*

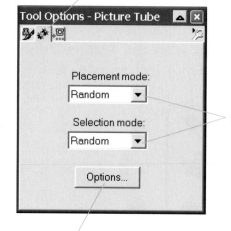

8 Select values in
these fields

9 Optional – click here for advanced
options, then follow steps 10–11

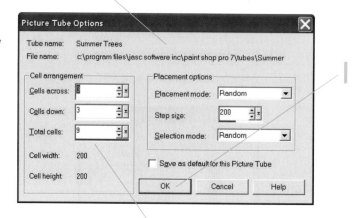

11 Click
here

10 Customise cell arrangement details
(but note the effect can sometimes
be undesirable)

12 Place the mouse pointer where you want the tube to start

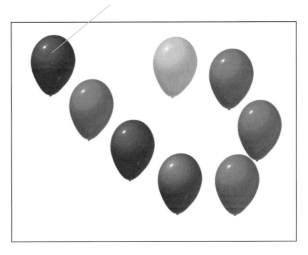

13 Drag with the left mouse button, then release it

Adjust the various settings to vary the effect – in the example on the right, different drag speeds have been used to control tube placement.

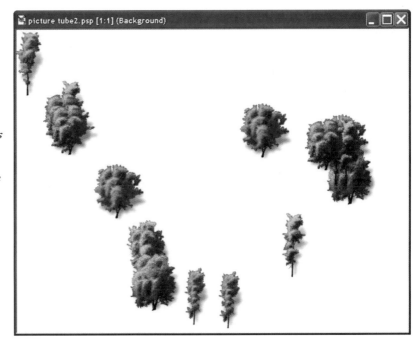

Drawing via the Preset Shapes tool

You can create shapes (e.g. complex vectors like hats, buttons, callouts or 3D spheres, or symbol-based vectors like arrows, circles and stars).

Using the Preset Shapes tool

Refer to the Tool palette and do the following:

Click here

2 Refer to the Tool Options toolbar and do the following:

Select Create as vector to define a vector shape, or deselect this to create a raster one.

3 Ensure this tab is active

4 Click here; in the list, select a shape

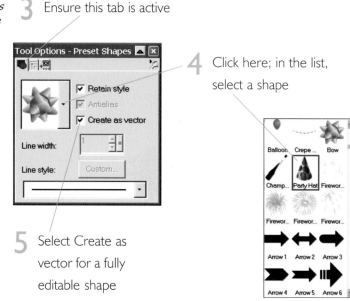

5 Select Create as vector for a fully editable shape

6 Drag with the left mouse button to draw the shape

When you've created a vector shape, you can save it to your own library for future use.

With the vector open, pull down the File menu and click Export, Shape. In the Export Shape Library dialog, name the vector. Click OK.

(To use the new shape, follow steps 1–6.)

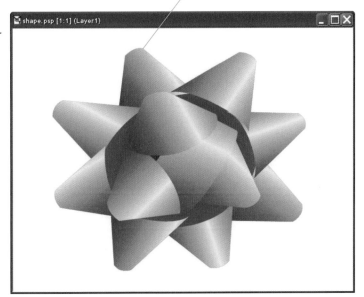

You can combine shapes quickly and easily to produce interesting effects.

Editing Preset shapes

To edit vector shapes/objects:

1 Refer to the Tool palette and do the following:

You can apply a new fill to vectors. Click the Styles/Fill box then do the following:

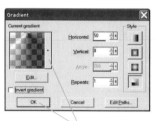

2 Click here

Click here. Select a new fill in the list, then click OK

A new fill has been applied

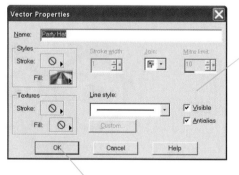

3 Double-click the vector

Re step 4 – depending on the vector selected, some of the options may be greyed out and therefore unavailable.

4 Complete the dialog fields (e.g. to amend the shape width, enter a new entry in the Stroke width field)

5 Click here

Node editing – an overview

Vector objects consist of a path with at least one contour. The more complex the vector, the more contours it has. Contours, in turn, consist of:

You should note that Paint Shop Pro has the following node types:

- *Tangent – allows curves and lines to blend invisibly*

- *Corner (or Cusp) – apart from dragging the node (see page 99), you can also drag the node handles independently (see page 102)*

- *Curve – produces very smooth curves (there are two sub-types: Symmetrical and Asymmetrical)*

- two or more nodes (control points)

- linking segments (straight or curved)

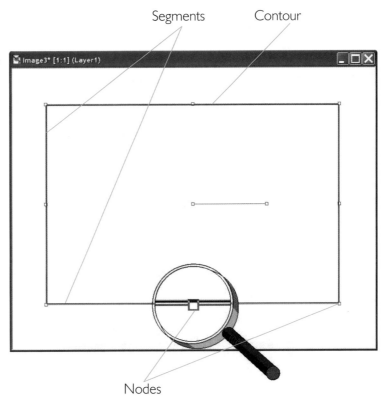

Editing (manipulating) nodes is carried out in a special mode called Node Edit. Node Edit mode:

- displays the vector's path

- does not accurately reflect the vector's true appearance

Only one path can be edited at once, but you can use nodes to reshape vector objects in an almost infinite number of ways.

Launching Node Edit mode

To enter Node Edit mode (preparatory to manipulating vector nodes), do the following:

1 Activate this button in the Tool palette:

2 Right-click the vector object you want to edit; in the menu, select Node Edit

To leave Node Edit mode, perform one of the following operations:

- *to leave Node Edit without applying any changes you've made, press Esc*

- *to leave Node Edit and apply any changes you've made, press Ctrl+Q. (Alternatively, right-click the vector and choose Quit Node Editing from the menu.)*

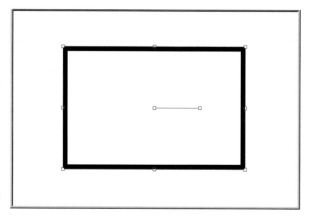

A selected vector object in normal mode

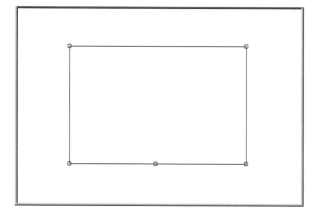

The same vector object in Node Edit mode

Node operations

You can create a new contour by adding a new node.

In Node Edit mode, press Ctrl+E. Left-click away from a segment. Now either:

• Left-click once to create a straight segment, or;

• Drag with the mouse to create a curved segment

Adding new nodes
In Node Edit mode, do the following:

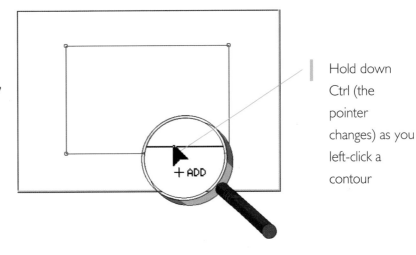

Hold down Ctrl (the pointer changes) as you left-click a contour

+ ADD

Moving nodes
In Node Edit mode, do the following:

You can also select multiple nodes by holding down Shift as you click them.

Dragging a segment rather than a node moves the entire contour.

If you've only selected one node, you can move it in increments of 45°. Simply hold down Shift as you drag.

1 Drag a marquee around 1 or more nodes to select them

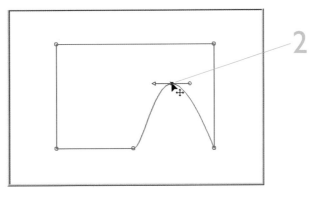

2 Drag the node(s) to a new location (thus warping the vector)

Changing a node's type

Applying a new type to a node has an impact on the segments which enter and leave it.

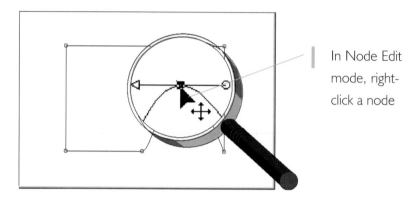

In Node Edit mode, right-click a node

2 In the menu, click Node Type. In the sub-menu, select a node type

Merging nodes

When you 'merge' a node, you delete it. This results in the two segments which enter it being united into one.

Follow step 1 above to select a node, then press Ctrl+M

You can merge multiple nodes. However, note the following caveats:

- *the effect can be hard to predict*
- *merging every node within a contour deletes the contour*

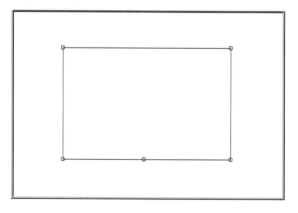

The illustration at the base of page 99, after the node flagged by step 2 has been merged

Breaking nodes

You can 'break' nodes. This means that the contour in which the node is situated is:

- split into two separate contours (if the original was open)

- opened out (if the original contour was closed)

To join nodes (contours), hold down Ctrl as you drag one node over another. When the pointer looks like this:

JOIN

release the mouse button.

| In Node Edit mode, left-click a node

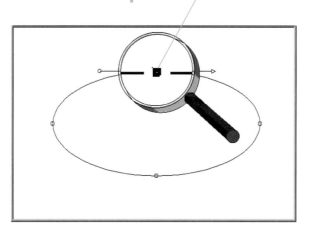

To copy a contour, select the relevant nodes then press Ctrl+C. To paste in the contour, press Ctrl+V. (The new contour is inserted with a slight offset.)

2 Press Ctrl +K then drag the nodes apart

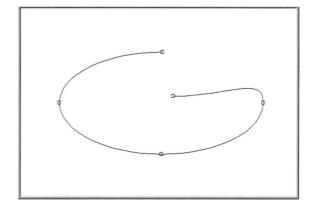

Here, the closed ellipse in the upper illustration has been opened

Using node handles

Handles are only visible in Node Edit mode.

Two handles extend from Asymmetric/Symmetric nodes. You can use these to redefine the shape of the host contour.

Node handles vary according to the node type. For instance, Cusp node handles move independently...

Hold down Shift to constrain the reshaping to 45° increments.

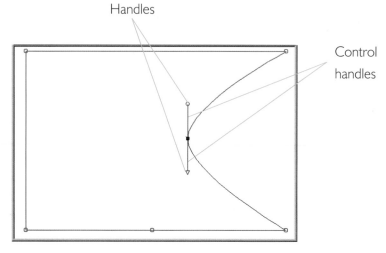

Drag a handle to a new location to reshape the contour

In the example below, the bottom handle has been dragged straight down:

Here, the fact that the node is Symmetrical has ensured that the upper handle has also moved an equal distance i.e. the control handles are equal in length. (With Asymmetrical nodes, the handles can vary in size.)

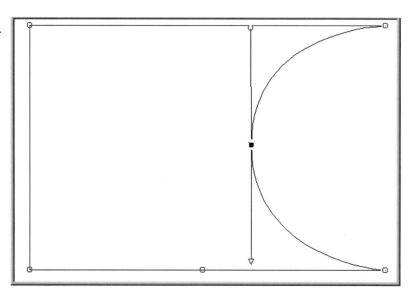

Using filters

In this chapter, you'll learn how to add a variety of creative effects to images (or image selections). You'll do this by applying any of Paint Shop Pro's numerous filters.

Finally, you'll create your own filters; amend user-defined filters; and apply these to images or image selections.

Covers

Chapter Four

Using filters

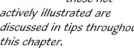

Paint Shop Pro provides numerous filters. Some of those not actively illustrated are discussed in tips throughout this chapter.

In Paint Shop Pro, the distinction between filters, deformations and effects is sometimes less than precise.

Note that filters only work with the following image types:

- *coloured images with more than 256 colours, and;*

- *256-colour greyscales*

Filters enhance images (or image selections, if you've pre-selected part of a picture) by varying the colour of every pixel ('picture element') in line with:

- its current colour

- the colours of any neighbouring pixels

You can also create and apply your own filters, for some really distinctive and original effects.

Applying a filter

1 If applicable, pre-select part of the relevant image

2 Pull down the Effects menu and click Effect Browser

3 Click a filter

4 Click OK

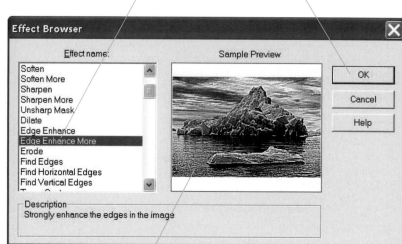

The change is previewed here

If the image you want to apply a filter to doesn't meet the criteria in the BEWARE tip, press Ctrl+Shift+0 (zero) to increase the colour depth to 16 million.

You can also use a menu route to apply filters. Pull down the Effects menu and make the appropriate choices.

5 Complete any additional dialog which launches – Paint Shop Pro applies the selected filter

Filter gallery

Experiment with applying more than one filter to images (or the same filter more than once) – the effects can be dramatic.

Paint Shop Pro ships with numerous filters. Some of the most useful are detailed in this chapter.

Compare this image (unchanged) with examples of filters below and later in this chapter

Use the Edge Enhance More filter (it works by amplifying edge contrast) to increase image clarity. (For a similar but reduced effect, use the Edge Enhance filter.)

Example filters

Edge Enhance More

Use the Find Horizontal Edges and Find Vertical Edges filters when you need to identify – and emphasise – those parts of an image which have significant horizontal or vertical colour transitions. (They work by darkening an image and then stressing the edges.)

Find Edges

Use the Find Edges filter (it works by darkening an image and emphasising its edges) to increase image clarity.

The Trace Contour filter is a specialist edge filter which, effectively, outlines images by defining a border around them.

Trace Contour

The Edge Preserving Smooth filter removes noise without loss of edge detail.

Edge Preserving Smooth

The Blur More filter lightens pixels which adjoin the hard edges of defined lines and shaded areas, making for a hazy effect. (For a similar but reduced effect, use the Blur filter.)

Blur More

You can also sharpen images (though in a different way) by using the paradoxically named Unsharpen filter.

 Paint Shop Pro offers more specialist filters. For example, use the Deinterlace filter to correct video images.

Ensure no selection area has been defined. Pull down the Effects menu and click Enhance Photo, Deinterlace. Complete the dialog, then click OK.

 The Sharpen More filter improves an image's focus and clarity. (For a similar but reduced effect, use the Sharpen filter.)

 The Add Noise filter ensures that images have randomly distributed colour pixels; you can determine, in a special dialog, the extent and type of the distribution.

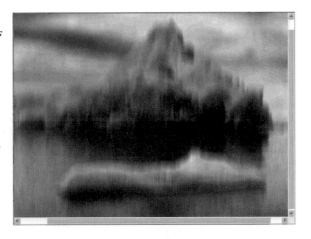

Motion
Blur

Sharpen
More

Add
Noise

The *Median filter reduces image noise by 'averaging' pixel brightness and discarding pixels which have relatively little in common with their neighbours.*

 Use the Blur Average filter to remove noise which is spread over the whole of an image.

Median

 The Dilate filter enhances light areas in an image.

 Use the Salt and Pepper filter to remove noise/specks (e.g. dust) from photographs. It works best when you apply it to a pre-defined selection.

Dilate

 Use the Despeckle filter to blur all of an image except those locations (edges) where meaningful colour changes take place.

 Use the Soften or Soften More filters to diminish image graininess.

Erode

User-defined filters

You can define your own filters, easily and conveniently. Once created, new filters can be named, saved and applied to images whenever required.

The next illustration shows an image before the application of a user-defined filter:

Paint Shop Pro provides some further examples of customised filters.

Press F1 to launch HELP. Click Help Topics. Click this tab:

Go to 'Example Filters'.

And now the result of applying the filter:

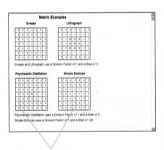

Sample filters

Working with filters

Defining your own filter

Pull down the Effects menu and click User Defined. Now carry out the following steps:

To apply a user-defined filter, pull down the Effects menu and select User Defined. In the dialog, select a filter and click Apply.

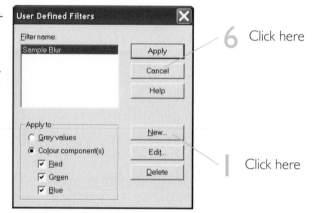

6 Click here

1 Click here

Slight amendments to any values in the Filter matrix can produce a marked effect.

2 Name the new filter

The settings shown in the matrix produce the effect shown on page 109.

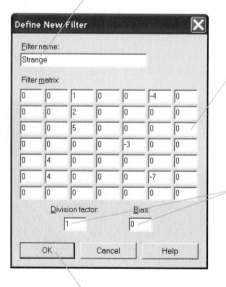

3 Enter the appropriate whole values (as plus or minus values)

4 Optional – amend the Division factor: and Bias: fields

5 Click here

Using deformations

In this chapter, you'll add additional creative effects to images (or image selections) by applying specialist deformations. Finally, you'll deform images on-the-fly, with the use of the mouse.

Covers

Chapter Five

Using deformations

Deformations enhance images (or image selections, if you've pre-selected part of a picture) by transferring data from one image area to another. This makes them more spectacular than filters.

Applying a deformation

Note that deformations only work with the following image types:

- *coloured images with more than 256 colours, and;*
- *256-colour greyscales*

1 If applicable, pre-select part of the relevant image or apply a mask (see Chapter 9 for more on masks)

If the image you want to apply a deformation to doesn't meet the criteria in the BEWARE tip, press Ctrl+Shift+0 (zero) to increase the colour depth to 16 million.

2 Pull down the Effects menu and click Effect Browser

3 Click a deformation   4 Click OK

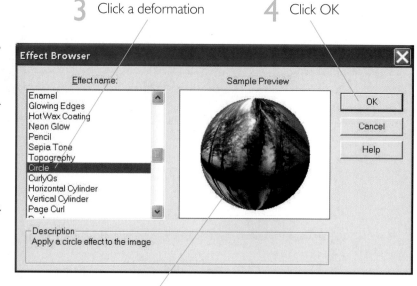

In Paint Shop Pro, the distinction between filters, deformations and effects is sometimes less than precise.

The change is previewed here

You can also use a menu route to apply deformations. Pull down the Effects menu and make the appropriate choices.

5 Complete any additional dialog which launches – Paint Shop Pro applies the selected deformation

Deformation gallery

Paint Shop Pro ships with numerous deformations. Some of the most useful are detailed in this chapter.

Compare this image (unchanged) with examples of deformations below and later in this chapter:

Example deformations: Circle

CurlyQs deformation

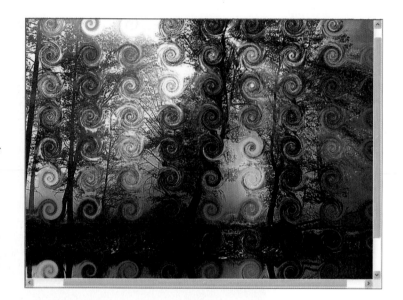

The CurlyQs deformation splits images into curled columns.

Horizontal Cylinder deformation

The Horizontal Cylinder deformation stretches an image

horizontally.

Vertical Cylinder deformation

 The Vertical Cylinder deformation stretches an image vertically.

Pentagon deformation

As implied, the Pentagon deformation transforms an image into a five-sided figure.

Rotating Mirror deformation

The Rotating Mirror deformation reflects part of an image on itself.

Horizontal Perspective deformation

The Horizontal Perspective deformation slants an image horizontally. (See also page 122.)

Vertical Perspective deformation

The Vertical Perspective deformation slants an image vertically. (See also page 122.)

Pinch deformation

Pinch compresses an image towards its centre.

Punch deformation

Punch imposes the opposite effect to Pinch.

Ripple deformation

Ripple defines concentric rings around an image's midpoint.

Twirl deformation

The Twirl deformation rotates an image around its centre.

Skew deformation

The Skew deformation slants images. (See also page 122.)

Spiky Halo deformation

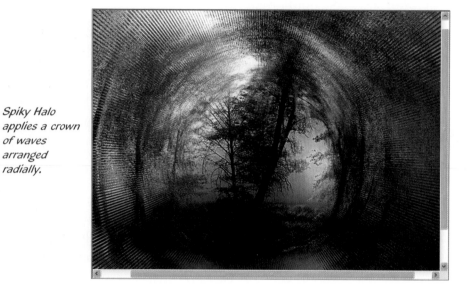

Spiky Halo applies a crown of waves arranged radially.

Warp deformation

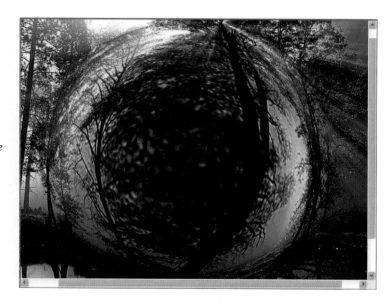

The Warp deformation magnifies an image's centre in relation to the remainder.

Wave deformation

The Wave deformation imposes undulating vertical and horizontal lines.

Wind deformation

Wind applies the effect of wind coming from the left or right.

Using the Deformation tool

You can deform images interactively, with the use of the mouse.

Deforming manually

Optionally, pre-select part of the image before step 1, to limit the deformation to the selection.

1 If you haven't created any layers, promote the standard Background to a layer (see the Hot TIP)

Re step 1 – right-click any toolbar and select Layer Palette in the menu. In the Layer Palette, right-click Background and select Promote to Layer.

2 Click this button in the Tool palette:

3 Drag a central handle to resize the image vertically or horizontally

Re step 3 – hold down Shift as you drag to skew the image.

Re step 4 – hold down Ctrl as you drag to change the image's perspective. Or hold down Ctrl and Shift to distort the image.

5 Drag the ends of the centre bar to rotate the image

4 Drag a corner handle to resize horizontally AND vertically

Re step 6 – if the Tool Options toolbar isn't on-screen, right-click any other toolbar. Choose Tool Options in the menu.

6 Click Apply to retain your changes or Cancel to revert to the original image

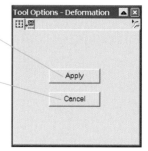

Using effects

In this chapter, you'll enhance images or image selections by applying any of Paint Shop Pro's numerous special effects. You'll also apply 3D effects to image selections and use specialised effects to enhance/correct photographs.

Covers

Chapter Six

Using effects

In addition to filters and deformations, Paint Shop Pro also provides numerous special effects. These are varied and include:

- artistic effects

- effects which impose textures

- effects which apply or reflect light

- effects to correct photographs (see pages 139-140)

Applying an effect

In Paint Shop Pro, the distinction between effects, deformations and effects is sometimes less than precise.

1 If applicable, pre-select part of the relevant image

2 Pull down the Effects menu and click Effect Browser

Note that effects only work with the following image types:

- *coloured images with more than 256 colours, and;*

- *256-colour greyscales*

- *(with certain effects) greyscales converted to 16 million colours*

3 Click a effect   4 Click OK

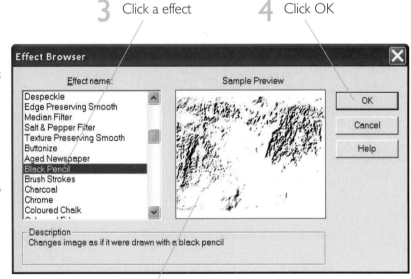

Effect Browser

Effect name:

Despeckle
Edge Preserving Smooth
Median Filter
Salt & Pepper Filter
Texture Preserving Smooth
Buttonize
Aged Newspaper
Black Pencil
Brush Strokes
Charcoal
Chrome
Coloured Chalk

Sample Preview

OK
Cancel
Help

Description
Changes image as if it were drawn with a black pencil

If the image you want to apply a effect to doesn't meet the criteria in the BEWARE tip, press Ctrl+Shift+0 (zero) to increase the colour depth to 16 million.

The change is previewed here

You can also use a menu route to apply effects. Pull down the Effects menu and make the appropriate choices.

5 Complete any additional dialog which launches – Paint Shop Pro applies the selected effect

Effect gallery

Experiment with applying more than one effect to images (or the same effect more than once) – the effects can be dramatic.

Paint Shop Pro ships with numerous effects. Some of the most useful are detailed in this chapter.

Compare this image (unchanged) with examples of effects below and later in this chapter

Some effects come with 'presets', ready-made formatting collections which give professional results. Apply presets in step 5 on page 124.

Example effects

Aged Newspaper mimics the effect of an ageing newspaper and resembles Sepia's (qv) 19th century mode. Apply Aged Newspaper to a greyscale image then convert it to 16 million colours.

Aged Newspaper

Black Pencil mimics the effect of drawing with a black pencil on a white background. Similar to Charcoal but has more detail.

Black Pencil

You can specify whether the blinds are horizontal or vertical.

Blinds

Brush Strokes makes images look like watercolours – experiment with the various presets.

Brush Strokes (the 'Water color' preset)

Charcoal is similar to Black Pencil but gives less detail.

Charcoal

Chrome mimics applying a metallic patina to images.

Chrome

Colored
Chalk

Colored Foil combines a sculpted look with multiple colours.

Colored
Foil

Colored
Edges

Colored
Pencil

Contours changes images into topographical maps (qv Topography).

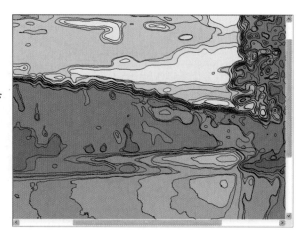

Contours

Dilate strengthens an image's light areas.

Dilate

Emboss transforms the image into a bas-relief (shapes project from the background without becoming detached). Colours are also inserted when appropriate.

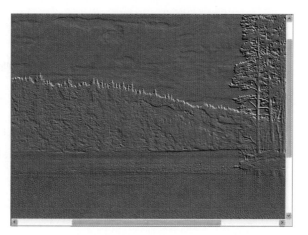

Emboss

Feedback makes an image appear to be reflected inwards in concentric mirrors.

Feedback

Fine Leather incorporates embossing.

Fine Leather

Fur makes an image appear 'bristly'.

Fur

Glowing Edges colours image edges in neon (other image parts are blackened).

Glowing
Edges

 Kaleidoscope mimics the effect of looking through a kaleidoscope.

Kaleidoscope

 Lights spotlights images – you can specify the number of spotlights. Here, a preset (Sunset) has been applied.

Lights

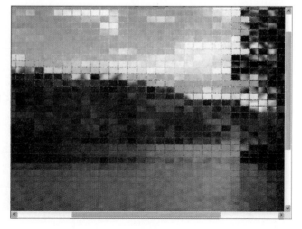

 Mosaic - Antique mimics applying antique tiles.

Mosaic - Antique

Neon Glow makes images 3D and emphasises edge contrast.

Neon Glow

You can specify the basic colour and which corner curls.

Page Curl

Pattern applies a geometric pattern to images.

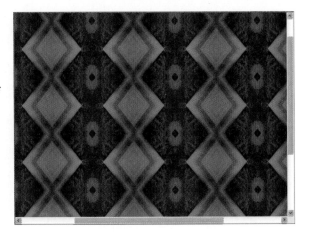

Pattern

Pencil – as well as making an image look like a pencil drawing – also colours the edges.

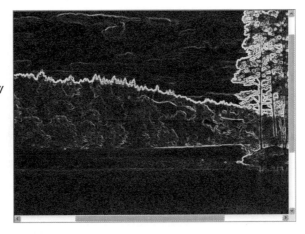

Pencil

 The Pixelate effect applies squares or rectangles (you can specify the size) to an image.

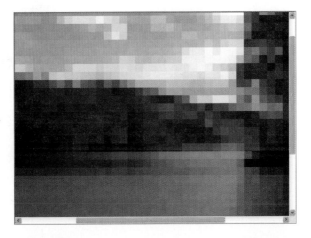

Pixelate

 Polished Stone makes an image look as if it's been carved out of a shiny surface.

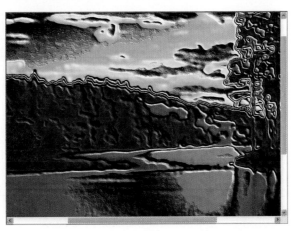

Polished
Stone

Rough Leather incorporates embossing.

Rough Leather

Sandstone

Sculpture stengthens an image's edges and applies a coloured pattern. You can specify the pattern or apply a preset.

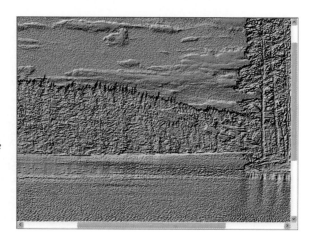

Sculpture

Sepia either makes an image look as if it was produced in the 19th century (greyscale an image then convert it to 16 million colours before applying the effect) or – as here – it gives it a more contemporary, 1940s feel (apply it to a 16 million-colour non-greyscale image).

Sepia

 To greyscale an image, choose Colours, Grey Scale.

 Soft Plastic mimics the effect of being constructed of plastic. Experiment with the various presets.

Soft Plastic

 Straw-wall simulates applying straws to an image.

Straw-wall

Sunburst simulates viewing an image and its source of illumination through a lens.

Sunburst

Texture mimics painting an image onto a textured surface. You can specify which texture is applied.

Texture

Tiles (default)

Tiles (Glass preset)

 Topography gives a 3D flavour to an image by applying consecutive terraces.

Topography

 You can specify the number of Weave strands and the colour of the gaps.

Weave

Using 3D effects

Paint Shop Pro also ships with several 3D effects which you can only apply to image selections. These include:

- Buttonize (very useful for websites)

- Chisel

- Cutout

- Drop Shadow

In the Anniversary Edition, most of these effects are not available from the Effect Browser.

Applying a 3D effect

1 Pre-select part of an image

2 Pull down the Effects menu and click 3D Effects. In the sub-menu, select the effect

3 Complete any further dialog which launches

A Web button

An image with drop shadow

Chisel makes an image appear to have been cut out of stone

Using photographic effects

You can use a variety of specialist filters to enhance photos. For example, you can:

For more on enhancements you can make to photos, see the DON'T FORGET tips on pages 167 and 170.

- remove red-eye (flash light reflected from the subject's retina onto the film)

- remove moiré (an undesirable blotchy pattern)

- automatically erase scratches

- compensate for fade

Applying a photographic effect

1 Pull down the Effects menu and do the following:

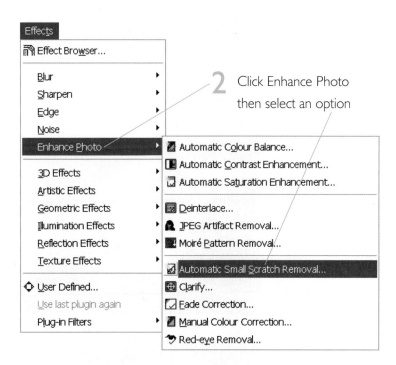

3 Complete any further dialog which launches.

Scratch removal in action

Scratches

This is an old photograph, so its quality is less than exceptional.

Apply photographic effects several times, watching carefully to make sure the remainder of the image doesn't suffer and fine-tuning the settings as required.

After several passes, the scratches are diminished

Using plug-ins

In this chapter, you'll enhance images or image selections by applying any of Paint Shop Pro's numerous special plug-ins.

Covers

Chapter Seven

Using plug-ins

The Anniversary Edition ships with a collection of third-party plug-ins which apply effects. Many of these are complete but a number are demonstration versions – this means that certain functions (usually presets) are disabled. With some plug-ins, even those that do work are stamped with 'DEMO...'.

All plug-ins are applied via idiosyncratic dialogs, of which the following is a representative sample.

Applying a plug-in

1 If applicable, pre-select part of the relevant image

Note that plug-ins only work with the following image types:

- *coloured images with more than 256 colours, and;*
- *256-colour greyscales*

If the image you want to apply a plug-in to doesn't meet the criteria in the BEWARE tip, press Ctrl+Shift+0 (zero) to increase the colour depth to 16 million.

2 Pull down the Effects menu and do the following:

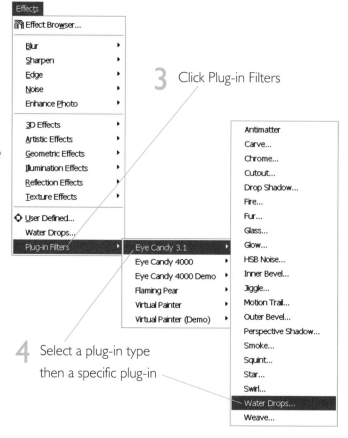

3 Click Plug-in Filters

4 Select a plug-in type then a specific plug-in

...cont'd

5 Drag any of the sliders
to customise the plug-in

7 Click here to
apply the plug-in

*This dialog is
only an
example —
complete the
relevant fields,
as appropriate.*

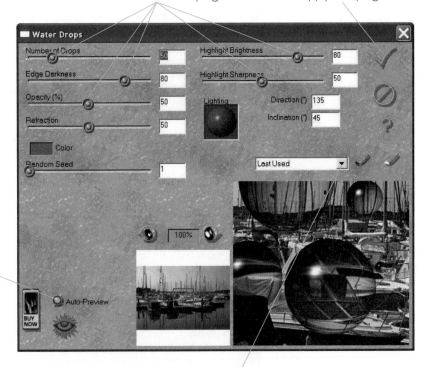

*If you want to
preview the
plug-in you're
using in the
actual image
(as opposed to the dialog),
select Auto-Preview.*

6 Optional – click here and
select a preset in the list

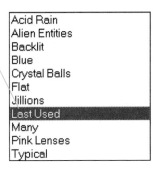

Some plug-ins in action

Some plug-ins take quite some time to apply.

Water Drops (Eye Candy 3.1)

Lacquer (Flaming Pear)

There are two fully functioning Virtual Painter plug-ins; both mimic artistic effects.

Collage (Virtual Painter)

Paint Shop Pro and the Web

In this chapter, you'll learn how to customise and export images for use on the Web. Techniques you'll use include rollovers, slicing and mapping. You'll also send pictures by email directly from within Paint Shop Pro.

Covers

Chapter Eight

Brief notes on image formats

Image formats supported by Paint Shop Pro are bitmaps (rasters), vectors and metas.

Bitmaps consist of coloured dots, while vectors are defined by equations (thus often giving better results with rescaled images). Metas are blanket formats which explicitly allow the inclusion of raster and vector data, as well as text annotations.

Paint Shop Pro recognises a wide selection of bitmap, vector and meta graphic formats. These are some of the main ones:

Bitmap formats

PCX	Originated with PC Paintbrush. Used for years to transfer graphics data between Windows application. Supports compression
TIFF	Tagged Image File Format. Suffix: .TIF. If anything, even more widely used than PCX, across a whole range of platforms and applications
BMP	Not as common as PCX and TIFF, but still popular. Tends to produce large files
TGA	Targa. A high-end format, and also a bridge with so-called low-end computers (e.g. Amiga and Atari). Often used in PC and Mac paint and ray-tracing programs because of its high-resolution colour fidelity. Supports compression
PCD	(Kodak) PhotoCD. Used primarily to store photographs on CD. Paint Shop Pro will not export to PCD
GIF	Graphics Interchange Format. Just about any Windows program – and a lot more besides – will read GIF. Frequently used on the Internet. Disadvantage: it can't handle more than 256 colours. Compression is supported
JPEG	Joint Photographic Experts Group. Used for photograph storage, especially on the Internet. It supports a very high-level of compression, usually without appreciable distortion
PNG	Interlaced Portable Network Graphics. Used occasionally on the Internet

Although Paint Shop Pro supports numerous image formats, the last three in the 'Bitmap formats' table are particularly suitable for Web use:

- *GIF (suitable for line art and images of 256 colours or fewer)*
- *JPEG (especially effective for photographs)*
- *PNG (suitable for most images, but not supported by all browsers)*

Vector formats

An example of a meta format is Windows Metafile (suffix: .WMF). This can be used for data exchange between just about all Windows programs.

CGM	Computer Graphics Metafile. Frequently used in the past, especially as a medium for clip-art transmission. Less frequently used nowadays
EPS	The most widely used PostScript format. Combines vector and raster data with a low-resolution informational bitmap header. The preferred vector format

Exporting files for the Internet

You can use steps 1–5 on page 18 to produce files suitable for Internet use. However, Paint Shop Pro makes it even easier to produce transparent GIF, JPEG and PNG files by providing specialised export dialogs.

Exporting GIF/JPEG/PNG files

1 Pull down the File menu and click Export

2 In the sub-menu, click JPEG Optimizer, GIF Optimizer or PNG Optimizer

3 Complete the dialog which launches (the dialog varies according to which option is chosen in step 2):

4 Activate each tab in turn, then complete the relevant options

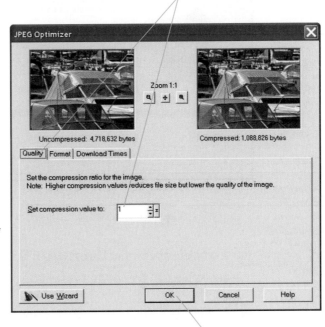

No browsers currently support layers. Therefore, before you export a layered picture for Web use, flatten it by pulling down the Layers menu and selecting Merge, Merge All (Flatten).

5 Click here

Exporting GIF/JPEG/PNG files – a simpler route

If you're unsure about completing all of the options when you export files for Internet use (and some of the options – particularly PNG – can be complex), you can use a shortcut:

Smaller file sizes work better on the Web (many users won't wait while large files download). So effective publishing on the Web involves getting the maximum compression while keeping image quality adequately high.

1 Follow steps 1–2 on page 147

2 Click this button in the dialog:

3 Complete the options

Some PCs are limited to 256-colour display. Images with more colours are 'dithered' and are often distorted. As a result, it's a good idea to reduce images you create for the Web to 256 colours (Ctrl+Shift+3).

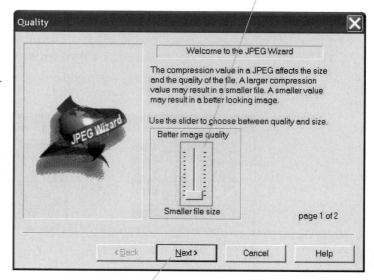

4 Click here

Ignore the Export, StudioAvenue. com entry in the File menu. JASC formerly offered users the ability to save up to 50Mb of pictures on a dedicated website. This service is currently unavailable.

5 Complete any further dialogs which launch (clicking Next where applicable to move on to the next dialog)

6 In the Final dialog, click Finish to complete the export process

Image slicing

To email the open image, choose File, Send. Paint Shop Pro opens your email client with the picture set up as an attachment.

You can use a technique known as image slicing to:

- save an image into smaller parts (in various formats/ specifications)

- reduce downloading time (by saving fewer image parts – those used repeatedly are only saved once)

1 Select the image you want to split

2 Pull down the File menu and click Export, Image Slicer

3 Click one of these, then click in the image preview

To delete a cell, do the following. Click this button in the dialog:

Now click the cell.

The Image Slicer works by dividing images into rectangles. You do this by applying grids (step 4) or lines (step 5).

When you've done this, you apply specific properties to the rectangles (cells) – see page 150.

4 If you selected [#] in step 3, complete the Grid Size dialog, then click OK

To preview your image in your Internet browser, click this button:

The image previewed in Internet Explorer 6 before the export settings are quite right

Re step 7 – in the Target field you can choose from the following options:

- _blank – the linked page opens in a new browser window
- _parent – the linked page opens in the parent window
- _self – the linked page opens in the same window as the link
- _top – the linked page opens in the full browser window

5 If you selected  in step 3, click and drag vertically over the image preview to create a vertical line, or horizontally to create a horizontal line

6 Click here, then click in a cell to select it (it's outlined in green after selection)

7 Complete the Properties section

8 Click in the Format box and select a format (e.g. GIF)

9 Click **Optimize Cell...** and complete the dialog which launches by activating each tab and selecting the relevant options in each

10 Click Close and complete any further dialogs

Using rollovers

You can also use Paint Shop Pro to export 'rollovers'. Rollovers are image sections which change into something else when activated and are often used on the Internet, particularly in website navigation bars.

The use of rollovers can make websites look much more graphically effective, and more professional.

Exporting rollovers

1 Follow steps 1–6 on pages 149–150

2 Click here

8 Click here

3 Perform steps 4–7 overleaf

4 Select the appropriate
initiating mouse action

5 Click the mouse
action's Open button

*Repeat steps
4–6 as often
as required.*

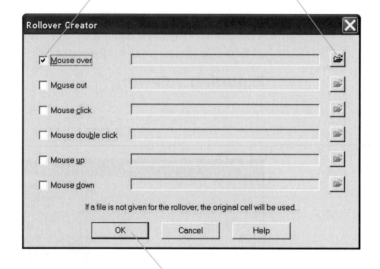

7 Click here

6 Locate and double-click the file you
want to associate with the rollover

Image mapping

You can use a technique known as image mapping to create image areas (hot spots) which are linked to Internet addresses (URLs):

1 Open the image you want to map and make it active

2 Pull down the File menu and click Export, Image Mapper

To delete a shape you've defined in step 4, do the following.

Click this button:

Now click the shape.

3 Click the Polygon, Rectangle or Circle tool, then click in the image preview

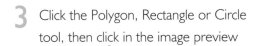

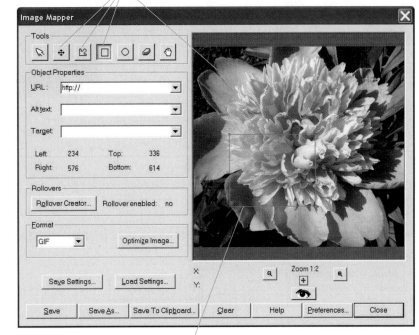

The Image Mapper works by dividing images into polygons, rectangles or circles.

When you've done this, you apply specific properties to the shapes – see page 154.

4 Drag out a map shape

5 Complete the additional steps overleaf

To preview your image in your Internet browser, click this button:

The image previewed in Internet Explorer

6 Click here, then click in a cell to select it (it's outlined in green after selection)

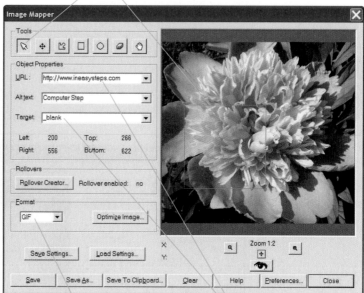

7 Complete the Properties section

Re step 7 – in the Target field you can choose from the following options:

- *_blank – the linked page opens in a new browser window*
- *_parent – the linked page opens in the parent window*
- *_self – the linked page opens in the same window as the link*
- *_top – the linked page opens in the full browser window*

8 Click in the Format box and select a format (e.g. GIF)

9 Click **Optimize Image...** and complete the dialog which launches by activating each tab and selecting the relevant options in each

10 Click Close and complete any further dialogs

Additional techniques

In this chapter, you'll learn how to apply borders/frames to images; carry out screen captures; work with layers; and apply/edit masks. You'll also create workspaces (so you can return more quickly to ongoing work) and use Autosave to guard against system crashes. Then you'll crop images; work with histograms to readjust colour values; and carry out other colour corrections (including Posterize/Solarize).

Finally, you'll convert images in batches, then preview – and print – your work (including multiple image printing and printing crop/registration marks).

Covers

Chapter Nine

Layers – an overview

Paint Shop Pro images are divided into 'layers'. Layers are separate, transparent levels which add a new dimension to image editing. Memory permitting, you can have as many as 100 layers.

There are three kinds of layer:

- raster (hosts pixel-related data)

- vector (holds vector objects e.g. shapes and text)

- adjustment (contains colour correction data)

Vector layers can be added to any image, but raster and adjustment layers can only be created in:

- greyscale images

- images with at least 16 million colours

Layer editing and manipulation are largely undertaken via the Layer palette. The Layer palette shows each layer and its sequence in the overall stack of layers. It also, in the case of a vector layer, displays icons representing each vector object:

You can paint (or apply effects to) specific layers. When you do this, unaffected areas in underlying layers remain visible until such time as you merge the layers.

Much of the usefulness of layers comes from the following:

- *making one or more layers temporarily invisible*

- *applying masks to layers (see later)*

To the left of the button which displays the layer name, Paint Shop Pro displays an icon showing what type of layer it is e.g.:

Bitmap

Vector

Background

The icon for Adjustment layers varies with the sub-type.

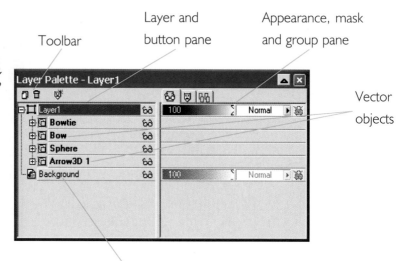

Toolbar

Layer and button pane

Appearance, mask and group pane

Vector objects

The Background (raster) layer – each new image has one

Adding new layers

You can use a shortcut to create a new raster layer (with default properties): hold down Shift as you left-click the button shown in step 1.

1 In the Layer palette toolbar (see the facing page), right-click this button:

2 Click a layer type

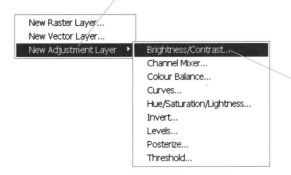

3 If you chose New Adjustment Layer in step 2, select a layer sub-type

4 Name the layer

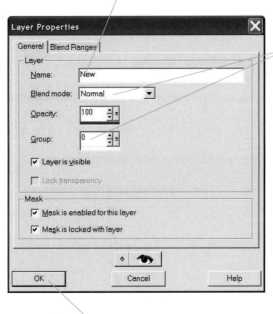

To launch the Layer palette, right-click any toolbar. In the menu, select Layer Palette.
(Or, as a shortcut, simply press L.)

5 Complete the other fields (they vary according to the layer type) or accept the defaults

6 Click OK

Using layers

Rearranging layers

1 If the Layer palette isn't on-screen, press L

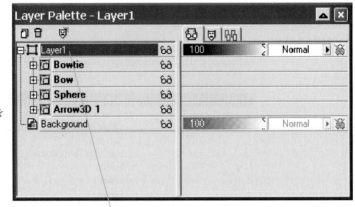

To delete a layer, right-click it in the Layer palette. In the menu which launches, click Delete.

2 Click a layer, then drag it up or down to a new location in the palette

3 Release the mouse button

Merging layers

When you merge layers, you join all the component layers (or simply all visible layers) into one. As a result:

By default, each image has a Background layer. To promote this into a normal one, right-click it in the palette. In the menu, select Promote To Layer.

- they can no longer be edited independently

- all vector objects are rasterised

- all transparent areas are whitened

Carry out ONE of the following, as appropriate:

To retain all layer information, follow the procedures in the HOT TIP on page 18 when saving your layered images.

However, note that you can also select 'Photoshop (*.psd)' in step 1 on page 18 since the Adobe Photoshop format also retains full layer details.

1 To merge all the layers within an image, pull down the Layers menu and select Merge All (Flatten)

2 To merge only those layers currently visible within an image, pull down the Layers menu and select Merge Visible

You can border images with the Background colour. You can border all four sides, or permutations.

Open the relevant image. Pull down the Image menu and select Add Borders. Now do one of the following:

- *in the dialog, leave Symmetric selected to border all sides, then enter a border thickness in one of the entry fields.*

- *alternatively, to only border specific sides, deselect Symmetric and enter a thickness in one or more fields.*

Finally, click OK.

Duplicating layers

1 If the Layer palette isn't on-screen, press L

2 Click a layer, then drag it over the button

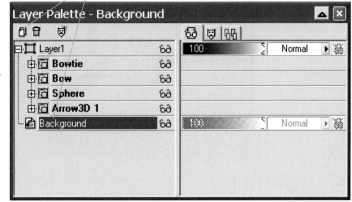

3 Release the mouse button

The result:

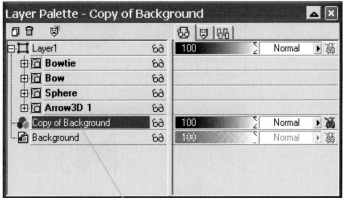

One frame option from the Picture Frame Wizard

The Background layer has been copied
(the new layer is named 'Copy of ...')

To frame an image, pull down the Image menu and click Picture Frame. Complete the Picture Frame Wizard dialogs.

Viewing layers

To re-display a layer, repeat step 2 but click this icon instead:

To view or hide all layers, pull down the Layers menu and click View, All or View, None respectively.

To make all invisible layers visible (or vice versa), pull down the Layers menu and click View, Invert.

Current (visible) layers which hold no data are transparent.

Hiding/showing layers or layer objects

If the Layer palette isn't on-screen, press L

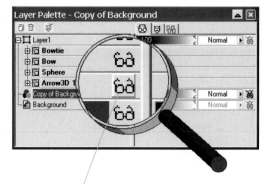

2 Click a layer's (or a vector object's)
Visibility button to hide it – the button changes to:

Here, 4 vector objects are shown, all on the one layer (Layer1)

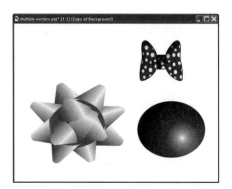

Now, step 2 has hidden the arrow...

Masks – an overview

The fact that masks are bitmaps means that all bitmap tools work with them.

Another corollary is that in those tools which have bitmap and vector modes (e.g. the Preset Shapes tool), only the bitmap component is operative on masks.

Masks are 256-colour greyscale bitmaps which are overlaid over image layers. They contain 'holes'; you perform editing operations on the areas displayed through the gaps. The holes can be created via:

• selection areas

• other images

Alternatively, the mask can be as large as the underlying layer.

To an extent, as we've seen, masks can be regarded as stencils. However, also implicit in the above description is the fact that they act as advanced selection areas. For example, you can control the extent to which a mask operates by defining the greyscale content:

— painting with black augments masking

You can apply any filter, deformation or effect which can be used with greyscale images.

— painting with white effaces masking

— any intervening shade of grey allows a portion of the effect you generate to take effect

In the illustration on the right, a separate image has been applied as a mask, and a fill applied.

image-mask.tif [1:1] (Background)

Layer masks

You shouldn't apply masks to a Background layer – instead, promote the layer first. (See the HOT TIP on page 158.)

You can create three principal types of mask:

- masks which apply to one specific layer

- selection masks (formed from, and based on, a pre-defined selection)

- image masks (based on a second image)

Masking an entire layer

If the Layer palette isn't on-screen, press L

Toolbar

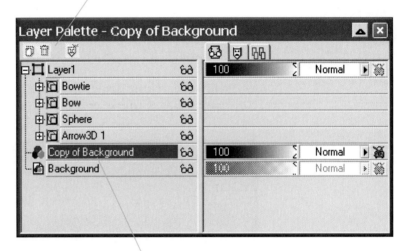

2 Select a layer

Re steps 3 and 4 – you can edit the mask later to mask selective areas.

3 Left-click this button: [🖼] in the Layer palette's toolbar – the entire layer is now masked

4 To unmask the layer, select it in the Layer palette. Pull down the Masks menu and click Delete. In the message which appears, click No to remove the mask entirely or Yes to incorporate it into the layer

Selection masks

When you create a mask, it's invisible. To view it, press Ctrl+Alt+V. (To hide it again, repeat this.)
  Viewed masks are coloured red:

Selection masks are masks which contain a hole (the hole being supplied by the selection area). By default, any changes you make apply to the hole, not the surrounding area.

Creating a selection mask

Define the appropriate selection area (see chapter 2 for how to do this). Now do the following:

1   If the Layer palette isn't on-screen, press L

Toolbar

A rectangular selection mask made visible

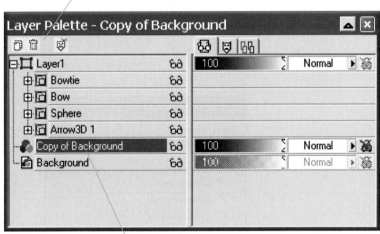

2   Select a layer

3   Right-click this button: 🛡 in the Layer palette's toolbar, then do ONE of the following:

After step 5, press Ctrl+D to remove the original selection area.

4   In the menu, click Hide Selection (to mask the selection)

5   In the menu, click Show Selection (to mask everything apart from the selection)

Image masks

Creating masks from other images is a very useful technique. It can produce quite remarkable effects.

Creating masks from images

1 Open the image you want to use as a mask

2 Open the image into which you want to insert the mask

3 In the destination image, follow steps 1–2 on page 163

4 Pull down the Masks menu and click New, From Image

5 Click here; in the list, select the mask image

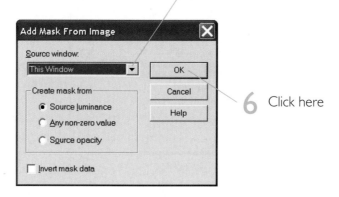

Add Mask From Image

Source window:
This Window

Create mask from
- Source luminance
- Any non-zero value
- Source opacity

☐ Invert mask data

OK
Cancel
Help

6 Click here

The result:

Pressing Ctrl+Alt+V has made the image mask visible.

One image (the helicopter) has been inserted as a mask

Editing masks

In particular, you can use the Fill tool to apply a new fill. (See page 161 for a description of how colours influence the efficiency of masks.)

Paint Shop Pro has a special mode in which you can edit masks. This can involve:

- varying the extent of the mask (i.e. by painting over the object)

- painting the mask to control the degree (if any) of masking

Amending a mask

1 To view the mask, pull down the Masks menu and select View Mask

2 To enter Edit mode, press Ctrl+K

Re step 3 – you should make use of the following as guidelines:

- *paint with black to add masking*
- *paint with white to remove the mask, or;*
- *paint with grey shades to apply differing mask levels*

3 Alter the mask with any of the painting tools

4 To leave Edit mode, press Ctrl+K again

Reusing masks

Paint Shop Pro lets you save a mask to disk, as a special file (with the suffix .MSK). You can then load it into a new image. This is a convenient way to reuse masks.

Saving a mask

Define a mask. Pull down the Masks menu and click Save To Disk. Now do the following:

Re step 2 – you may have to activate one or more folders first, to locate the folder you want to save the mask to.

It's probably best to use 'Masks', which Paint Shop Pro creates on installation:

Click here. In the drop-down list, click a drive

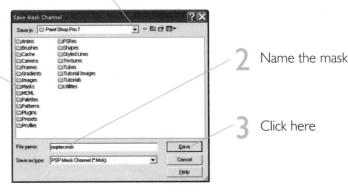

2 Name the mask

3 Click here

Loading a mask

Pull down the Masks menu and click Load From Disk. Now do the following:

Click here. In the drop-down list, click a drive

Re step 2 – you may have to activate one or more folders first (e.g. \Program Files\Jasc Software Inc\Paint Shop Pro 7\Masks) to locate the folder which hosts the mask you want to open.

2 Select a mask

3 Click here

Screen captures

In programs (like Word 2002) which support OLE (Object Linking and Embedding), you can capture screens without having already started Paint Shop Pro.

In the OLE-compliant program, activate the 'Insert Object' command (usually Insert Object in the Insert menu). In the dialog, activate the Create New tab/ feature and double-click Paint Shop Pro 7 Screen Capture. Follow steps 1–3 on page 168, then click OK. Go to the screen you want to capture and follow step 4 in the table.

The captured screen is inserted into the OLE-compliant program.

You can have Paint Shop Pro create a snapshot of all or part of any Windows screen.

You can:

- specify which part of the screen is captured

- specify the signal which initiates the capture. You can use:

    — a keystroke combination (known as a 'hotkey') e.g. F11 or Alt+F1

    — the right mouse button

    — a specific interval (in seconds) instead of a trigger

- include the cursor in the capture

Having Paint Shop Pro perform a screen capture consists of the following stages:

Step 1	Arrange the screen appropriately (this includes making the program whose screen you want to capture active)
Step 2	Switch to Paint Shop Pro
Step 3	Tell Paint Shop Pro to initiate a capture (at which point it minimises)
Step 4	Issue the capture signal
Step 5	Return to Paint Shop Pro (the captured screen automatically occupies its own window) and perform any necessary editing actions (e.g. cropping or converting to greyscale)
Step 6	Use standard procedures to save the screen capture as a graphics file for later use

You can correct fade (the process by which light distorts the colours) in photographs .

Pull down the Effects menu and click Enhance Photo, Fade Correction.

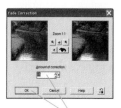

Type in a correction amount (in the range 1–100) then click OK

Re step 2 – you can dispense with allocating a trigger and, instead, tell Paint Shop Pro to begin the capture process so many seconds after you carry out step 4.

Simply omit step 2 and select Delay timer. Now insert the relevant interval into the box below Delay timer.

Re step 3 – carry out this step if you want to capture the cursor e.g.:

Paint Shop Pro's Zoom cursor

(You can't capture the cursor if you selected Area in step 1.)

Performing a screen capture

Perform steps 1–2 in the table on page 167. Pull down the File menu and click Import, Screen Capture, Setup. Do the following:

1 Select a region   2 Optional – select a trigger

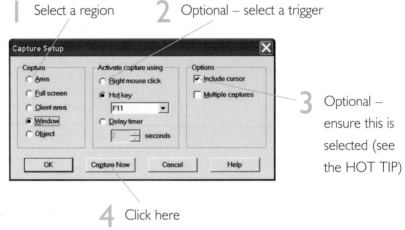

3 Optional – ensure this is selected (see the HOT TIP)

4 Click here

Paint Shop Pro minimises, and you're returned to the application whose screen you want to capture. Now perform ONE of the following:

5 If you selected Area, Object, Window or Client area in step 1, place the cursor over the screen component you want to capture

6 If you selected Full Screen in step 1, place the cursor anywhere on the screen

Follow step 4 in the table on page 167. Additionally, if you selected Area in step 1 above:

7 Position the cursor at one corner of the area you want to capture. Left-click once, then place the cursor at the opposing corner and left-click again

Back in Paint Shop Pro, perform steps 5–6 on page 167, as appropriate.

Colour corrections – an overview

You can 'crop' images. This means defining an area you want to keep and discarding the rest.

Define the relevant selection area, then press Shift+R.

Alternatively, activate the Crop tool in the Tool Palette:

Define the relevant selection area, then double-click inside it.

Paint Shop Pro lets you make various adjustments to image colour distribution. To help you decide which amendments are necessary, you can call up a special window: the Histogram viewer. Look at the illustrations below:

The original image

You can use the Crop tool (see the above tip) to adjust the crop area you've just defined.

- *to move (but not resize) the crop rectangle, click inside it and drag to a new location, or;*
- *to resize the rectangle, move the cursor over one of the sides or corners, then drag in or out*

Spike

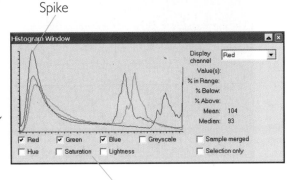

... and its histogram (to launch the Histogram window, press H)

Here, the RGB (Red/Green/Blue) components have been selected

You can also display greyscale, hue, saturation and lightness values by ticking the relevant box(es).

The Histogram window displays, along the horizontal axis, the three RGB components (Red, Green and Blue). The vertical axis against which these are plotted represents each component's share of colours in pixels.

The far left of the horizontal axis represents black, the far right white. Spikes indicate a concentration of a particular value (e.g. Red).

Histogram functions

To invert an image (convert its colours to their opposites), pull down the Colours menu and click Negative Image.

You can carry out two principal histogram-based operations on images: Equalize and Stretch.

Equalize rearranges image pixels so that those around the midpoint of the relevant histogram are pushed nearer the high and low brightness levels (see page 169 for more information). The result is normally an averaging of image brightness.

Stretch has somewhat the opposite effect. In images where black and white are not included in the histogram, it ensures the colours do span the full spectrum.

Applying Equalize or Stretch

If appropriate, define a selection area. Pull down the Colours menu and click Histogram Functions, Equalize OR Histogram Functions, Stretch.

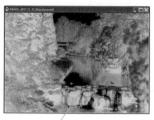

The original image, inverted

An unchanged image

... and after applying Equalize

To carry out a variety of further colour adjustments (e.g. amend brightness/contrast), pull down the Colours menu and click Adjust, followed by the relevant sub-option. Complete the dialog which launches, and click OK.

You can also automate the process to some extent. Choose Enhance Photo in the Effects menu, then click Automatic Colour Balance, Automatic Contrast Enhancement or Automatic Saturation Enhancement. Complete the dialog and click OK.

Solarize

Solarize inverts (reverses) colours which are over a user-set luminance threshold.

Paint Shop Pro has two further functions which manipulate image colours: Solarize and Posterize.

The illustration below shows the effect of applying the Solarize effect to the original image on the facing page:

To Posterize an image (where you specify an image's brightness value so that the result amounts to a special effect), pull down the Colours menu and select Posterize. In the dialog, amend the Levels field (in the range 2–255, where 2 produces the maximum effect). Click OK.

Solarizing an image

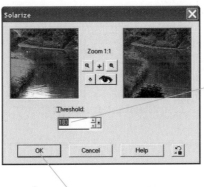

Posterize in action (maximum effect)

Setting the threshold at 1 is the same as inversion (see the HOT TIP on the facing page).

1 Optional – to restrict the effect, define a selection area

2 Pull down the Colours menu and select Solarize

3 Adjust the Threshold entry to the required setting – the permitted range is 1 (maximal effect) to 254 (minimal effect)

4 Click here

Using workspaces

You can save details of:

- toolbar and palette placement (i.e. whether they're docked or floating and – if floating – where they are on screen)

- grid and ruler settings

- which images are active and where their files are stored

- current zoom settings

as a 'workspace' file to disk. Paint Shop Pro gives the files a .WSP extension.

The advantage of this procedure is that you can quickly and easily return to a previous configuration of Paint Shop Pro, simply by loading the appropriate workspace file.

You should note the following when you create a workspace:

- *Paint Shop Pro prompts you to save any previously unsaved (and therefore unnamed) images*

- *Paint Shop Pro automatically saves any previously saved images which have since been amended*

- *the workspace save only stores details of where the relevant files are located, not the files themselves (this means that if you move or delete any of the files, they will not be present when you reload the workspace)*

Saving workspaces

1 Pull down the File menu and click Workspace, Save

2 Select a drive/folder

3 Name the workspace

4 Click Save

In chapter 1, we looked at saving images to alternative formats. This is a way of converting images, but one at a time. However, Paint Shop Pro lets you convert multiple images in one operation, a great saving in time and effort.

Pull down the File menu and click Batch Conversion. Use the Batch Conversion dialog to:

- locate the files you want to convert

- select them (hold down Shift and click to select ranges)

- select an output format

- (optionally) customise the output format (by clicking the Options button and completing the resultant format-variable dialog)

- select an output folder

Click Start to perform the conversion. When Paint Shop Pro tells you conversion is complete, click OK.

Recently saved workspaces can also be loaded via a menu. Pull down the File menu and click Workspace. In the sub-menu, click the workspace entry.

Loading workspaces

1 Pull down the File menu and click Workspace, Load

2 Select a drive/folder

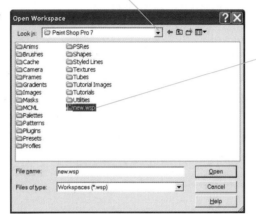

3 Double-click a workspace

Deleting workspaces

1 Pull down the File menu and click Workspace, Delete

2 Select a drive/folder

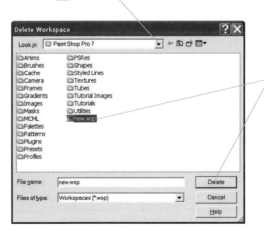

3 Click a workspace then click Delete

Using Autosave

If Windows or Paint Shop Pro crash suddenly, you run the risk of losing much or all of your work. However, you can prevent this by activating Paint Shop Pro's Autosave feature. When active, Autosave stores temporary details of active images. After any crash, Paint Shop Pro searches for these when you restart it. If it finds them, it reloads the temporary images.

Activating Autosave

Pull down the File menu and click Preferences, Autosave Settings.

Select Enable autosave

To deactivate Autosave, deselect Enable autosave.

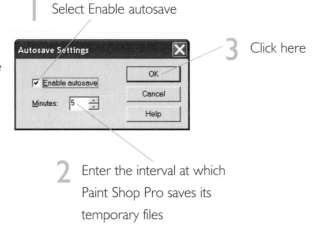

3 Click here

2 Enter the interval at which Paint Shop Pro saves its temporary files

By default, Paint Shop Pro saves its temporary files in your \WINDOWS\TEMP folder. However, you can change this if you want.

Specifying a new temporary file location

You'll have to restart Windows before this change takes effect.

1 Pull down the File menu and click Preferences, File Locations

2 In the File Locations dialog, activate the Undo/Temporary Files tab

3 In the Location of undo/temporary files box, type in the new folder address then click OK

Using Print Preview

To specify page setup settings, click this button in the toolbar:

Setup...

Make the relevant amendments in the Page Setup dialog. For example:

- *to print in greyscale (not colour), select Greyscale*
- *to centre the image, select Center on page*
- *to print lengthways, select Landscape*
- *to select a page size, click in the Size field; in the list, select a size*
- *to use another printer, click Printer and select it in the new dialog*
- *to print CMYK separations (for commercial printing – consult your printer first), tick CMYK separations*

Finally, click OK.

You need to ensure you print images with the correct resolution. Use the following guide:

- *300 dpi (dots per inch) printing – image resolution 72–120*
- *600 dpi printing – image resolution 125–170*

To set an image's resolution, use the Resize dialog (page 14)

Paint Shop Pro provides a special view mode called Print Preview. This displays the active image exactly as it will look when printed. Use Print Preview as a final check just before you print your image.

You can customise the way Print Preview displays your image by zooming in or out on the active page. You can also specify page setup settings.

Launching Print Preview

Pull down the File menu and click Print Preview. This is the result:

Print Preview toolbar

Zooming in and out in Print Preview

1   To zoom in (increase magnification), click this button: Zoom In
Repeat if necessary

2   To zoom out, click this button: Zoom Out   Repeat if necessary

Printing

You can arrange and print multiple images on a single piece of paper.

Open the relevant images. Pull down the File menu and click Print Multiple Images. In the special screen:

do the following:

- *drag images from the bar on the left onto the correct page location (as here)*
- *(optionally) click an image and apply any relevant menu commands (e.g. to view information about the image, select Image Information in the Image menu...)*
- *finally, to print the images pull down the File menu and click Print*

To print to a file (e.g. for submission to a commercial printer), tick Print to file. Follow step 9, allocate a name in the dialog and click OK.

When you've previewed your image and it's ready to print, do the following:

Printing your work

1 Pull down the File menu and click Print (or press Ctrl+P)

2 Click here; select a printer

3 Optional – click here to adjust your printer's settings (and see its manual)

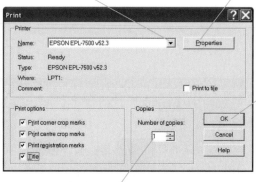

9 Click here

4 Type in the no. of copies you require

5 To print corner crop marks, tick Print corner crop marks. This option (and the two in steps 6–7) helps commercial printers ensure print and colour accuracy, and mainly applies to PostScript output (the Encapsulated PostScript filter – see page 18). If you're printing to a desktop printer, you won't need these features

6 To print centre crop marks, tick Print centre crop marks

7 To print registration marks, tick Print registration marks

8 To print the filename – or any title entered in the Current Image Information dialog (see page 12) – tick Title

Paint Shop Pro starts printing the active image.

Animation Shop

In this chapter, you'll learn how to create animated images and banners for use on websites. You'll also customise completed animations by adding transitions, effects and text effects to individual frames; inserting new frames; resizing animations; and optimising them for Web/presentation use.

Finally, you'll export frames directly to Paint Shop Pro (so you can make use of its more advanced editing capabilities) and preview your animations in your Web browser prior to uploading.

Covers

Chapter Ten

Creating animations

You can use a companion program called Animation Shop to animate images. This is fun and useful, particularly as you can create animations for websites.

Creating an animation

The easiest way to create animations is to use a special wizard.

Animations consist of frames (images) viewed successively. Therefore, you should use the wizard to create the frames you need. (But be prepared to create quite a few – broadly, the more frames, the better the result.)

1 Pull down the File menu and select Animation Wizard

2 There are several stages in the wizard (complete each screen and click Next to progress):

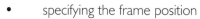

Animation properties include the ability to have animations 'loop' (play continuously).

- specifying the frame size
- specifying the canvas colour
- specifying the frame position
- specifying animation properties
- adding new frames

If in doubt, stick with the wizard defaults.

3 In the final screen, click Finish

4 To run your animation, select Animation in the View menu

An animation in the course of being run

Creating an animated banner

You can create banners with animated text – great for use on the Web.

To insert a new blank frame into an existing animation, click the frame you want the new frame to precede or follow then press Ctrl+T or Ctrl+Shift+T respectively.

To insert a frame with content, choose Animation, Insert Frames, From File. In the dialog, click Add File and select one or more animation files. Click Open. Complete the remainder of the Insert Frames from Files dialog then click OK.

1 Pull down the File menu and select Banner Wizard

2 There are several stages in the wizard (complete each screen and click Next to progress):

- specifying the background
- specifying the size of the banner
- specifying the timing
- specifying the text colour
- specifying a transition

To launch JASC's Browser from within Animation Shop, press

Ctrl+B.

3 In the final screen, click Finish

4 To run your animation, pull down the View menu and click Animation

You can also run animations by clicking this button in the on-screen

toolbar:

Computer Step for great computer books!

Frame 4 of 10

A completed banner

Working with frames

Transitions control how the animation moves from one frame to the next. Effects manipulate frames in dramatic ways – many of Animation Shop's effects are similar to those in Paint Shop Pro itself (e.g. Pixelate) but there are additions (e.g. Shaky Cam).

Applying transitions always results in new frames, while effects can add or amend frames – see below.

Once you've created an animation, you can customise it. This principally involves selecting individual frames and applying or modifying transitions or effects.

Applying transitions and effects

Right-click a frame

F:2 D:10   F:3 D:10   F:4 D:10

Inserting transitions or effects adds the specified number of frames to the animation.

However, you can also 'apply' effects. Essentially, this substitutes the changes you make in the specified number of frames. To do this, choose Apply Image Effect in step 2 then complete the dialog.

In the menu, select
Insert Image
Transition or Insert
Image Effect

You can also insert or apply text effects. Follow step 1. In 2, select Insert Text Effect or Apply Text Effect. Complete the dialog which launches in line with steps 7–8, but additionally enter the text you want to add. Complete step 9.

3 Complete steps 4–6 for transitions, or 7–9 for effects

...cont'd

It's sometimes appropriate to have the start or end of a transition as a colour rather than a frame. If you want this, click Canvas Colour under Start with or End with. Or click Custom Colour, click in the box and select a colour in the dialog.

You can export frames directly to Paint Shop Pro for editing there. Right-click a single frame or a group of pre-selected frames (to select several frames, first activate the Arrow tool:

then hold down Shift as you left-click them). In the menu, select Export Frames To Paint Shop Pro – Paint Shop Pro launches if it isn't already open. Make any editing changes then choose Update Back to Animation Shop in the Edit menu.

It's sometimes appropriate to have the start of an effect as a colour rather than a frame. If you want this, click Canvas Colour under Start with. Or click Custom Colour, click in the box and select a colour in the dialog.

Customising the transition

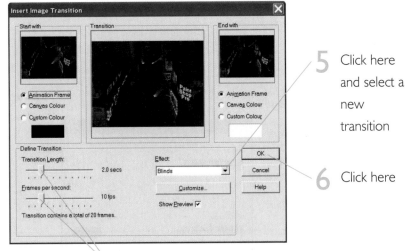

5 Click here and select a new transition

6 Click here

4 Drag the sliders to amend the transition duration and the frames per second value

Customising the effect

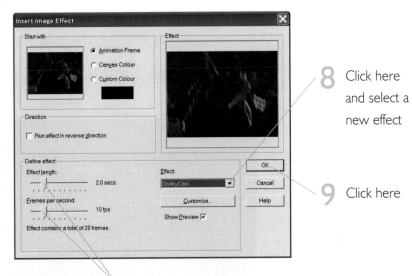

8 Click here and select a new effect

9 Click here

7 Drag the sliders to amend the effect duration and the frames per second value

Previewing animations

Since animations are especially useful on the Web, it's handy to be able to view them in your browser before uploading.

Animation Shop supports workspaces – see pages 172–173.

If you intend to use your animations on Web pages or in presentat-ions, you can run a special wizard to optimise them.

Choose File, Optimization Wizard. Complete the Wizard screens (some of them are identical to processes carried out by the Animation Wizard), clicking Next to move on to the next and Finish at the end.

1 Finish creating and modifying your animation, then choose Preview in Web Browser in the View menu

2 Select a format

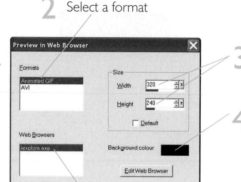

3 Optional – amend the size

4 Optional – click here and select a background colour in the Colour dialog

5 Select a browser then click Preview

6 Complete the remaining dialogs, as appropriate

You can resize animations. Press Shift+S then complete the Resize dialog. Be careful how much you resize: too much can distort images and text.

Internet Explorer previewing an animation

Media Center Plus Anniversary Edition only

In this chapter, you'll learn how to organise and manage your media files, using this useful utility supplied with Paint Shop Pro Anniversary Edition. You'll create albums (collections of thumbnails representing media files) and save them to disk, then export them to galleries for use on the Web. You'll also learn to add new files to existing albums; add keywords/comments to help you locate files; and work with thumbnails themselves.

Finally, you'll export media files for editing in their originating program and send files as email attachments from within Media Center Plus.

Covers

Chapter Eleven

Creating albums

You can save an album (or pre-selected media files in it) as a gallery of Web pages (in HTML format), a sort of ready-made website.

Choose File, Export, HTML. Complete the Export to HTML dialog (e.g. select a HTML design, pick a destination folder and specify which files to include). Click OK to build the gallery.

To preview the gallery in your browser, double-click the new HTML file.

You can merge albums. First, open the album into which you want to insert another album. Choose File, Merge, Saved Album. Use the Merge Album dialog to locate an album and double-click it to insert its files into the first.

You can expand existing albums at any time. Press F7 to add further files, or F8 to scan individual folders. In either case, complete the dialog which launches.

There is no Undo command in Media Center Plus.

If you're using the Anniversary Edition, you can use another companion program – Media Center Plus – to manage and publish media files. Media Center Plus defines media files as image, audio or animation files. The first step in using Media Center Plus is creating an album.

Creating an album

1   Press Ctrl+N

2   Optional – name the album (this isn't the file name – it's purely descriptive)

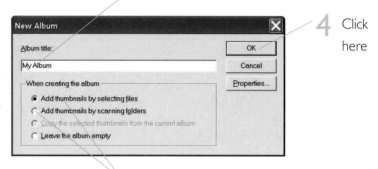

4   Click here

3   Specify how image thumbnails are added to the album

5   Complete the dialog which launches (specify individual image files for inclusion or pick a folder for Media Center Plus to scan, according to which option you selected in step 3)

Saving your album

1   Press Ctrl+S

2   Complete the Save As dialog (albums have the extension: *.alb)

Working with albums

You can also insert comments. In step 1, select Comments and do the following:

Enter comments and click OK

You can work with albums in various ways.

Adding keywords

When you create an album, Media Center Plus generates thumbnails for each relevant image. You can allocate descriptive keywords to thumbnails, so you can find them again more easily.

| Right-click a thumbnail and select Keywords in the menu

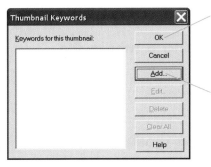

3 Click here

2 Click here; in the Add Keyword dialog, enter 1 or more keywords and click OK

You can run media files as a mini-presentation. Choose View, Run Slideshow. Slides should progress automati-cally – if they don't, press Spacebar (or Backspace to reverse the direction). To end a show, press Esc.

Searching for keywords

| Press Alt+F3

To search for comments, press Shift+F3. Type in the comment you want to search for and click Find First or Select All.

2 Enter keyword(s) and click Find First or Select All

To search for specific file names, press Ctrl+Shift+F3. Type in the name you want to search for and click Find First or Select All.

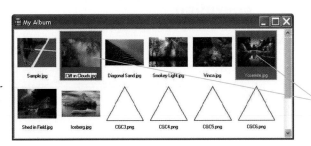

An album with thumbnails flagged after Select All was chosen

Working with thumbnails

To select more than 1 thumbnail, hold down Ctrl as you click them.

Before you print media files, carry out the following procedures:

- *select File, Page Setup. Complete the Page Setup dialog (e.g. select a page orientation and a paper size) then click OK*
- *select File, Print Preview to proof your files. Press Esc when you've finished (or Print to print directly)*

You can send a media file via email. Select the file's thumbnail and choose File, Send. Complete the Send dialog and click OK. Your email client opens a new email with the selected media file as an attachment.

To remove a thumbnail from an album (but without deleting the file itself), right-click it and select Delete from Album. (There is no warning before deletion.)

You can carry out various operations after right-clicking an image's thumbnail.

Viewing or playing a media file

Choose Play/View in the menu – press Esc when you've finished

Printing thumbnails/media files

Choose Print in the menu – complete the (standard) Print dialog

Converting a media file

Choose Convert in the menu – complete the Save to Media File As dialog

Editing a media file

Choose Edit Using in the menu. In the upper part of the sub-menu, click the suggested editor (shown in shorthand e.g. 'anim' for Animation Shop)

2 After editing is complete, back in Media Center Plus choose Edit, Update Thumbnails

Renaming a media file

Choose Rename in the menu – complete the Rename File dialog

Performing a copy-and-paste or cut-and-paste operation

Choose Copy or Cut in the menu

2 In another album, press Ctrl+V to paste in the copied media file

Index

D

E

F

G